W9-BVQ-259

DR. WILLIAM R. WIDGER, JR.
RFD #2, Hillrise Lane
Meredith, N. H. 03253

THE NEW SCIENCE OF ECONOMICS

AN INTRODUCTION

PREMIER BOOKS ARE DESIGNED TO BRING TO A LARGER READING PUBLIC OUTSTANDING BOOKS AT SMALL COST

GEORGE SOULE

THE NEW SCIENCE OF ECONOMICS

AN INTRODUCTION

Completely revised and expanded edition of
INTRODUCTION TO ECONOMIC SCIENCE

A PREMIER BOOK
Fawcett Publications, Inc., Greenwich, Conn.
Member of American Book Publishers Council, Inc.

A Premier Book published by arrangement with
The Viking Press, Inc.

Copyright 1948, © 1964, by George Soule
All rights reserved, including the right to reproduce
this book or portions thereof.

Library of Congress Catalog Card Number: 64-15059

This is a completely revised edition, expanded by about 80
percent, of INTRODUCTION TO ECONOMIC SCIENCE, 1948.

First Premier printing, July 1965

Premier Books are published by Fawcett World Library,
67 West 44th Street, New York, New York 10036
Printed in the United States of America

FOREWORD

Introduction to Economic Science, the book on which this revised and expanded edition is based, was published in 1948. Its purpose was to make as plain as possible how economic ideas were being tested and supplemented by careful research of a sort which could discover in quantitative terms and objective facts what lay beneath the surface of economic behavior.

Like workers in any respectable science, some economists had dedicated their efforts to candid, careful, and detailed observation and explanation of what in fact occurred. My book was a brief and nontechnical description of their methods and of the more important conclusions then possible. It was intended not for experts but for anyone interested.

Apparently many were interested, since sales of the 1948 book, including subsequent paperback printings, have totaled about a half-million copies.

Since 1948 economic experience and empirical analysis of it have enriched economic thinking. Understanding of the business cycle has been enlarged, since the passage of the Employment Act of 1946, by reports of the President's Council of Economic Advisers, of the Joint Economic Committee of Congress, and by the work of nongovernmental agencies—the National Bureau of Economic Research, university and other research institutions (see Chapter 4).

Though many forecasters have been deluded and economic prediction is still dangerous, a successful experiment in scientific forecasting has been made (see Chapter 5). Fluctuations of the business cycle have been dampened (see Chapter 9).

The recent interest in economic growth has led to the gathering of new facts and to new understanding. Advance in productivity and its influence on wages, prices, and employment have been analyzed. Such analysis permits a realistic view of automation and its horrible effects (see Chapters 8 and 10).

International affairs, both in practice and by analysis, have offered new insights to economic scientists. The Marshall Plan and the subsequent disappearance of the "dollar shortage," the remarkable postwar recovery of Western Europe and Japan, the formation of the European Common Market, have all occurred since 1948. They are discussed in Chapter 11, as is recent worry about the deficit in the international balance of payments of the United States and the consequent loss of gold.

The last chapter, 12, marshals some of the scientific contributions to answers of questions about the future. When, if ever, will the Soviet Union catch up with the United States in production? What is the cost to this country of competitive armament? What could be done with the resources which would be available if disarmament could be achieved, and what would be its effect on employment?

The same chapter discusses new economic discoveries about "investment in human beings" as an indispensable basis of gains in production. It suggests new and more rewarding goals for international rivalry if the arms race could be ended. And it suggests need for a new application of economic principles if automation should lead to further reduction in working hours —what about the economy of time-spending?

Additions to the original edition of the book have nearly doubled its length (they are about four-fifths as large as the original).

I am indebted to Arthur F. Burns, President of the National Bureau of Economic Research, for most of the material in Chapter 9, based in large part on his presidential address to the American Economic Association in 1961. Solomon Fabricant, Director of Research of the National Bureau, read, and suggested minor changes in, the section on productivity in Chapter 10, which is based on his analysis. Geoffrey Moore of the National Bureau read carefully and made valuable suggestions on Chapters 4 and 5, which are largely concerned with his work on the business cycle and forecasting. I have also made extensive use of the work of two other economic scientists of the

National Bureau of Economic Research—Hal Lary on the United States foreign balance of payments in Chapter 11, and J. Warren Nutter on comparative economic growth of the United States and the Soviet Union in Chapter 12. To all these economists I am indebted. None of them, however, can be held responsible for my opinions.

G. S.

CONTENTS

THE NEW SCIENCE OF ECONOMICS

AN INTRODUCTION

ONE

ECONOMIC FUNDAMENTALISM

While science has tremendously increased man's power over other things, his ability to direct his own conduct has not kept pace with his command of physical forces. Human society has difficulty in achieving aims which are generally regarded as desirable. So wide has become this disparity between man's control over nonhuman nature and his control over himself that many doubt whether the race can escape self-destruction.

Responsibility for this unhappy state of affairs is often placed upon science itself. Modern man, some believe, has devoted too much time to learning about cold and impersonal facts by processes of logic and too little to the spiritual and moral elements of human life. Those who adopt this view are inclined to regard the pursuit of science as a blind alley, in so far as human happiness is involved. Useful though it may be in adding to material comforts and conveniences or the arts of war, its achievements are now as embarrassing as would be a Diesel locomotive or a machine gun in the hands of a child in a nursery. The assumption of those affected by the reaction against science is that what mankind needs now most of all is not more knowledge or more skill, but more virtue.

This attitude is nowhere more prominent than in pronouncements by extreme conservatives about economic policy. They seem to believe that true economics is not an experimental science in the modern sense of the word, but a set of principles and maxims discovered once and for all in former centuries. Like Sunday-school teachers in a slum, they bid us return to the classical gospel, so that the balance of prices and production which is supposed to emerge from unrestricted operation of the laws of supply and demand under free enterprise may prevail. The world is all but lost; not a nation in it, with the possible exception of the United States, clings to the faith, and even here false prophets have led us astray. But to these authors, the truth is clear and whole. They seem to believe that we have wandered from the truth only because we did not understand. Patiently they explain it to us all over again, often in words of biblical simplicity. Once more they convict us of sin in a score of public policies, all the way from collective bargaining to compensatory spending by government.

The major admonitions of the conservatives are often as unassailable as the Ten Commandments. In judging the wisdom of any course of action, for instance, we should think not only of its effect on those whom it is supposed to benefit, but of its effect on all others as well. And we should think not only of its temporary result, but of its ultimate consequences. Applying these principles, one has no difficulty in proving that destruction does not add to economic welfare but robs us of wealth; that the ultimate good of workers, as well as of everyone else, depends upon improvement of productivity, even though technological advance may throw some out of work; that we cannot gain in the long run by obstructing imports or by giving away exports; that simply adding to the money supply does not make us rich; that inflation is an abomination; and that high taxes to support governmental activities may contribute less to the public welfare than would the same money spent in private enterprises.

These and other axioms of the same sort are universally accepted by economists as well as by sensible folk untrained in the subtleties of theory. To the economic preacher, it seems that the policies he opposes could be advocated only by persons ignorant of these principles or persons who ignored them. Indeed, few economists of any school would support a general policy of limitation of output, or make-work rules by unions, or opposition to mechanical improvement, or inflation, or the abandonment of saving, or governmental squandering of money. The unwary should not conclude that those who deplore the economic revivalist's position are not respectful of his main principles or disagree with his conclusions at every point. But they do disagree that letting things alone will produce the desired results.

What actually is the matter with the school of reasoning which is thus content to return to orthodox first principles?

Why has it seemed necessary to review not the aims, but the application, of the classical concepts?

The Fallacy of Concealed Premises

The first fallacy may be called the fallacy of concealed premises. In the classical economic writers it was masked by an oft-repeated phrase—*ceteris paribus,* other things being equal. For the sake of clarity, attention was concentrated on a single chain of cause and effect, while the writer assumed that nothing else in the field of forces changed or differed from his assumptions. Sometimes these assumptions were stated, often they were merely implied. But in the real world "other things" do not remain the same, and often differ so far from the assumptions of the writer that, if they are taken into account, they upset his conclusion. No good scientist thinks any more of cause and effect as a single chain; science now thinks in terms of a field of forces and of events in that field.

An example first invented by Bastiat and repeated in a book by Henry Hazlitt[1] is an excellent illustration of this fallacy. The breaking of a show window is welcomed by the crowd in the street because the replacement of the window will supply employment. The crowd forgets that the fifty dollars which the merchant must spend for the new window otherwise would have been spent for a new suit, which also would have furnished employment. The community has lost one window or its equivalent, and nothing can compensate for that fact. Labor will be diverted from making suits to making windows. This parable is then applied to explode the belief that war, despite its destructiveness, brings economic benefits.

Now, as a matter of fact, World War II *did* cause increased employment, as everybody, including Hazlitt, would have to admit if he had his eye on the facts rather than on the theory. Not only that, but in spite of the immense destruction which sopped up so much labor and materials, the goods consumed by the population were, as a whole, larger in quantity than in the years before the war, when unemployment was prevalent.

The trouble with the story about the broken window lies in its unstated and assumed premises. It assumes that the

[1] *Economics in One Lesson* by Henry Hazlitt (New York: Harper and Brothers, 1946).

merchant would spend his fifty dollars for a suit or something else if he did not have to buy the window. It assumes that he could not buy the suit and the window too, either by taking the extra money from under the mattress or borrowing it from a bank. It assumes, furthermore, that everybody is already employed, so that labor could not make the new suit if the window had to be made. In the case of the war, the assumptions were all contrary to the facts. The United States did not spend all it could until it had to spend for destruction. The extra money required could be borrowed. There were millions of unemployed, whose potential labor was being wasted until they were put to work as a result of war demand.

The lesson is not that we should favor war for economic reasons, though when we look at the whole picture, instead of just part of it, it is easier to see why people on occasion believe destruction will benefit them. The lesson is that we should learn how to use our productive capacity without war. Hazlitt is content merely with the axiom that destruction is destruction.

The Fallacy of Missing Quantities

It is characteristic of the popular preachers of classical economics that they often don't take the pains to see what bearing statistical facts have upon their conclusions. Of course, statistics can be misinterpreted, and some statistics are inaccurate representations of the facts they are supposed to report. Statistics should be handled with conscience and care. Nevertheless, the truth emerges not from contempt for facts, but from respect for them as a means of discovering the actual behavior of the economic world. Your devotee of traditional theory, on the contrary, begins by deducing his principles from a few simple premises. Then he "interprets" the statistics in the light of the "basic principles" he has "learned." Now, in any respectable science a theory deduced from postulates is regarded not as the final truth but as a hypothesis to be tested by experience or observation. Its logic may be perfect, granted its assumptions, but still it may not be an accurate representation of nature. Good theory is not independent of the behavior of nature. All scientific laws are, to be sure, simplified abstractions, and variations are almost always discovered in applying them. But careful study of such variations is always in order, because they may indicate flaws in the hypothesis or may involve such large aberrations as to show that the "law" is irrelevant to the real world. Selecting statistics to prove a hypothesis, or interpreting them on the basis of learned principles, is not the method of scientific discovery. Science has more respect for facts than that.

The example of the broken window is an instance of the error which may result from inattention to statistics. An illustration of their misuse to prove a preconceived dogma has to do with railway wages in the United States. It is a basic principle of classical economics that high prices restrict demand. A frequent inference from this principle is that high wages (wages being regarded as the price of labor) diminish the demand for workers and so reduce employment. To support this conclusion, it is pointed out that in recent years the number of railway workers has gone down while their wages per hour have risen. But nothing is said about the great increase in output per man-hour on the railways, another statistical fact of first importance. This held in check unit labor costs while hourly wages rose; it has made possible the handling of an increasing amount of railway transportation with fewer men. And nothing is said about the competition with railroads by motor truck, automobile, and aircraft. One cannot account for decreased railroad employment without considering a dozen other factors.

The Fallacy of Omitted Factors

The omission of relevant factors may be regarded as a special case of the concealed premises, but it is so important and so characteristic of the school of economic fundamentalism that it is worth separate mention. In applying principles to concrete cases—not merely in formulating them, mind you—the writers of this school ignore the kind of economic world we live in. They assume without further ado that perfect competition exists, that prices and production respond readily to demand, that the more efficient competitors will survive, that labor and capital are highly mobile. This sort of assumption is the basis of their general conclusion that intervention by government or unions is, as a rule, both unnecessary and harmful and that socialism is bound to be less efficient than private enterprise. Occasionally they admit exceptions, but these exceptions are not taken seriously in arriving at their recommendations.

Though your popularizer of classical "law" disapproves restriction of output and price-rigging in general terms, he seldom takes seriously a major development of American economic history—the growth of concentration of business control, its effect on irregularity of production and on price rigidity, its power as a pressure group, its influence on the volume of investment, on the growth and distribution of the national income. Maybe our economy acts just as if competition were as prevalent, and shifts of capital and labor as easy, as Adam Smith thought they ought to be. Or, to be fair, maybe our economy would act in this way if only government, organizations of labor, and other pressure groups would stop interfering. But it is hazardous to assume so without even mentioning monopoly and monopolistic competition. This is only one example of the total disregard of many important factors, such as recurrent depression and chronic unemployment.

The Fallacy of Separate Pieces

Modern science does not proceed merely by analyzing separate little pieces of its subject and then by pulling out one of the pieces to apply to a particular problem of practice, forgetting the rest. It not only strives to put the pieces together, as in a picture puzzle, but it also sees that the whole picture has an organic meaning which is more than a collection of its parts—a "Gestalt."

Nobody could be more wholehearted than the opponent of governmental deficits in describing the evils of inflation. Yet he denounces price-control and rationing when demand for important products greatly exceeds the supply—as it did for several years after the end of World War II. He seems to detect no inconsistency in these two positions. The opposition to price-control is based on the argument that a free interplay of prices and profits will lead to the most efficient satisfaction of demand. Yet the description of inflation shows clearly that this does not happen when inflationary forces are at work. Why does it not occur to him that price-fixing and rationing may be employed to moderate inflation? He just doesn't put them together.

Your economic fundamentalist is firm about the desirability of increasing production, and indicates that he knows it has increased in the past and may increase in the future. Yet any enlargement of the volume of purchasing power at any time, whether by governmental borrowing or credit expansion, seems to him "inflationary." When he discusses such measures he assumes that the extra spending will never increase production but only boost prices. But during a slump we may have idle capacity and unemployed labor. At such a time, might not a larger volume of spending employ them without raising prices? This possibility he never considers; he does not bring the two ideas together. He grossly misrepresents the compensatory-spending school by implying that what they want is rising prices. Government spending, he assumes, will always divert production from private channels, never increase its total.

If he paid more attention to recorded experience, he might see the necessity of putting his pieces together.

The Fallacy about Human Behavior

Underlying every other defect of the economic preacher's view is his misunderstanding of human motivation. It never seems to occur to him to ask why, in spite of the fact that Adam Smith attempted in 1776 to instruct people how they should organize human activities, and on the whole did a better and more celebrated job than has since been done, the economic behavior of the world is, by his standards, more iniquitous than ever.

Perhaps motives are different from those assumed in the classical analysis. For some reason the experience of people does not lead them to accept the approved recommendations. Can we rely on an individualistic society to pursue self-interest by competition and ingenuity and hard work, and to stop pursuing it by combinations, restrictions, demands for hand-outs and special favors? Hundreds of thousands of farmers will not resignedly accept bankruptcy when deflation hits them. When a 1932 arrives, fifteen million unemployed workers will not passively wait for the slow working out of automatic equilibrium by the kind of economic regime which produced their distress.

We may cheerfully admit that no matter what prompts human beings to act as they do, informed and intelligent persons ought not to support remedies which will make things worse instead of better. But is it not the responsibility of the scientist who aspires to influence conduct to find out how and why the real world behaves as it does, instead of sitting off and offering preachments to it which are seldom accepted? We do not lecture the steel which fails to withstand strain and stress when bridges tumble down. In such a case we dig not merely into our mathematics but into the surrounding forces and the properties of the materials with which we have to work.

Not Less Science, but More

The remedy for man's failure to control his own behavior lies not in abandoning science for dogma but in more and better science. This is not disparagement of virtue. Goodness is needed, and so are codes of ethics. But neither can help much without realistic understanding. If expositors of economics want to preach, they should be sure that they are able to recommend a feasible and beneficial mode of conduct. The kind of economics preached by the economic revivalists is not based upon a mature enough science to be of much use.

During the past fifty years economics as a science has taken a long leap ahead. It has been enabled to do so not because economists in general have become more clever, or because those few economic geniuses who have appeared tower over their predecessors as does a Newton or an Einstein. It has done so mainly because for the first time in history economists have been provided with large-scale and reasonably accurate access to the facts of economic behavior. They have begun to learn from the world of nature, like any normal scientist, instead of merely from a few scattered observations and imagined instances as in the more remote past.

During World War I an enormous amount of statistical material, hitherto inaccessible, began to be gathered in connection with the process of governmental control which was found necessary. In subsequent years compilation of such facts was continued and expanded, both by government and by private organizations. Research agencies, bent upon a scientific approach, strove to put this material in order and interpret it. The depression of the 1930s, followed by World War II, accelerated the process.

For a time it looked as if the meaning of the facts was being forgotten or overwhelmed in the mere bulk of the statistics turned up. The mine was operating full speed, but the huge piles of ore were not being smelted and turned into the desired instruments of thought and control. The scientific economic workers were regarded by some of their more elegant and gentlemanly colleagues who dealt in traditional abstractions as grimy and dim-visioned miners, grubbing in dark shafts and piling up mountains of ill-assorted facts without contributing to any broad view. But the work went on and presently meaning began to be introduced. There are now many ways in which the statistical ore may be put to use.

The process is a long way from being completed yet, but it has gone far enough so that at least it ought to be reported. Much is known that was unsuspected by those who wrote when economics was more a philosophy than a science. The new knowledge, and the possibilities of using it, cannot be explained in quite such neat and elementary syllogisms as the parables of primitive economics. Nevertheless, like any body of scientific knowledge, it is worth some effort to master. Lay readers have waded through hundreds of technical pages about discoveries of physics—such as relativity and atomic energy—which are far more difficult, and less capable of use by the citizens in the process of conducting their businesses or casting their votes. The purpose of this book is to explain something of the new science of political economy.

TWO

KEEPING BOOKS FOR ALL THE PEOPLE

Of all the recent advances in economic knowledge, none is capable of being put to more uses than the studies of the national income. Before these figures were available, it was impossible to tell with any accuracy whether the people of a nation were becoming worse or better off in a material sense, or, if there was progress, what the rate of progress was. Obtaining that information is far from exhausting the uses to which national income figures can be put. They show also what is happening to the various industries, to farmers, wage-earners, property owners, professional people. They are indispensable in making federal budgets or levying taxes. If the tax authorities know roughly how large an income we have and how it is distributed, they can much better calculate the yield of any income tax. Finally, the figures are capable of being put to use in planning for the future, as we shall see in later chapters.

Before it is possible to understand how the national income figures are used, it is necessary to know what they are and something about how they are obtained and put together.

Figures for the national income, past, present and future, appear frequently in the newspapers. So commonly accepted is the term that most people do not realize that it is comparatively new, and that they do not know exactly what it means. Before 1919 there were no good figures for the size of the national income in the United States or for its change from year to year. Nobody knew in detail how it was composed or how it was shared. Even the word itself was not carefully defined. During the period between the wars, laborious work by statisticians and economists gradually developed the idea and gave it substance.

Much of the pioneer work was done by the staff of a nongovernmental research agency, the National Bureau of Economic Research. Later the United States Department of Commerce took over the job and subsequently revised its tabulations. There are gaps in the basic data; estimates have to be made, and the final totals include a margin of error. Yet the several investigators in the field arrive at substantially similar results, and for many practical purposes the figures are accurate enough. Certainly they are far better than unsupported guesses. They are often particularly useful in following changes over a period of time.

Anybody who wants to know the basic facts about an economic enterprise consults a report of its operations prepared by accountants. National income accounting applies similar methods to the affairs of all the people in a nation. The total national income is usually stated in figures of so many billions that they lose meaning to persons accustomed to count their incomes in hundreds or thousands. But these enormous totals are far from the whole story. The businessman who inspects the financial report of a corporation does not stop when he looks at the figures of gross or net income. He also inspects the columns carefully to see how these figures were derived. Likewise, the totals of national income are what emerge after detailed calculations which in themselves reveal some of the most significant facts about the economy.

It has been said that study of the national income is the branch of economics which corresponds to anatomy in the study of the human body. Anatomy reveals the structure of the organism. It shows the size, composition, and interrelationships of its various parts. Anyone who knows anatomy can go on to study how these parts operate and how they develop. The study of living processes is called physiology. Classical economics attempted to describe the physiology of economic processes before the facts of economic anatomy were known. It talked about the relationship among prices, demand and supply, the functions of saving and capital, the operation of markets and similar subjects, but it talked about them in a world of abstractions. That is one reason why its conclusions often seem so remote and difficult to apply.

Of course, we must have an economic physiology if we are to understand and control our institutions, but we are able to develop a much better physiology now that the major facts of economic anatomy have become known and roughly measurable.

What the National Income Is

What exactly is meant by the national income? In a sense this term is a figure of speech, since the nation as a whole does not have an income which could be put down on an income-tax return, as is the income of an individual or a corporation. The national income is not, for instance, what a nation earns above its expenses by buying and selling abroad. It is estimated by a process of social accounting which regards the population of a nation as a unit. It is thought of as the sum of all incomes.

Now let us see how the reckoning of the national income looks for a given year, let us say 1961 (Table 1). At the beginning, for simplicity, it is better to list only the major totals, as derived from the most readily available figures.

Any skeptical person who looks carefully at this table may think of some other source of money which ordinarily would be regarded as income. What about allowances paid by parents to their sons and daughters, or scholarships awarded to students? What about the large amounts of philanthropic grants? What about inherited legacies?

Such payments—and others that might be added—are not payments for current production; they do not involve buying and selling. They are, rather, what is called "transfer payments"—purchasing power which is passed from the donor to the recipient without involving any production of goods and services on the way. When the student spends the scholarship money to pay his tuition, grocery bill, etc., these sums do enter the flow of national income and are counted under the headings listed. The donor has merely transferred some of his purchasing power to be put to economic use by the recipient.

Income Equals Product

Simon Kuznets, one of the greatest American authorities on the subject, defines the national income as "the net product of, or net return on, the economic activity of individuals, business firms, and the social and political institutions that make up a nation."

There lurks in this definition an extremely important equa-

TABLE 1. INCOME RECEIVED (1961)

(Billions of Dollars)

First we have the compensation of employees	302.2
Next there is the net income of independent business or professional men, such as doctors, small businessmen, or partners	34.7
Income of proprietors of farms was	13.7
Many people receive income from rent, and this must be listed	12.3
And we must not forget the profits of corporations (part of this is distributed and part is not, but both parts must be counted)	45.6
Finally, there is the net interest received by individuals	20.0
Since nobody receives income from any other source for current production, the total is the national income	427.8[1]

[1] There are certain statistical refinements employed in deriving these figures from the raw data, which may be of interest.

The compensation of employees includes not merely what they receive directly in wages and salaries, but indirect payments by their employers, such as contributions for social insurance or pension funds and compensation for injuries.

Profits of business as here listed exclude change in the value of inventories arising from shifts in prices. Such changes do not really constitute income, in the sense of something produced.

The figures given for business profits are for the profits *before* payment of taxes on that income. While the owners of the business do not retain that part of the profit which is taken by the government in taxes, it is part of the national income.

The figure for rental income which people receive includes not merely payments from tenants, but an estimate of the net rental value of houses occupied by their owners. Use of the houses is a substantial part of the owners' real income, and is so regarded in our government's social accounting.

The item for interest does *not* include interest received on government bonds. While people actually receive this money, it does not represent current production for the most part, since the debt was incurred mainly for war. To include this interest would make the postwar income seem larger than it is, in terms of actual product.

Finally, as noted, there are certain payments received, called transfer payments, which are not included in the national income. These are payments for which no services are currently rendered, and consequently do not represent production—payments such as old-age pensions, unemployment benefits and gifts.

tion. The national income is the net product of economic activity. At the same time, it is the net return from economic activity. In other words, the amount paid for everything that is produced for sale to final users is equal to the sum of the incomes of all the people. This equation, as will be explained later, leads to important conclusions.

It is easier, at the beginning, to see why output equals income if we think of income in physical terms. We spend our dollars for loaves of bread, houses, automobiles—these things constitute our real income. We can buy what the nation produces and no more, no matter how many dollars we may collectively have. In the case of services, such as those performed by lawyers, teachers, or doctors, the service output is obviously the same as the service income of the recipients. The barber, let us say, produces one haircut; at that moment the customer receives one haircut.

Suppose we do not spend some of our dollars for either goods or services but save them. Might not our total money income, in that case, be larger than the total value of the nation's product? The answer is no, not at any given moment. Where did we get the money? It came from somewhere along the course of production, and it was added into the value of the product. Of course, goods may remain unsold; their prices may have to be reduced. But if that happens, it changes the money incomes of the producers at the same time.

Income has to be stated in dollars rather than in goods if we are to deal in totals at all, since houses, loaves of bread, and automobiles cannot be added together to produce a total which means anything. Attach their prices to them, and it is possible to get the sum.

Another definition of the national income, supplied by the Department of Commerce, calls it "the aggregate earnings of labor and property which arise from the current production of goods and services by the nation's economy." This definition immediately goes on to recognize the fact that income equals product by adding, "Thus, it measures the total factor costs of the goods and services produced by the economy." "Factor costs" is a term used in economics to mean the costs of the factors which are needed for production—traditionally, the amounts required to pay for land or natural resources, labor or other services, and capital. In other words, what is paid out for production must necessarily equal the income of those who share, directly or indirectly, in the process of producing. For example, total wages are the income of labor; but if we think of the cost of the product, they are also the total cost of labor.

National Product

The income received in 1961 is listed on a previous page. A substantially different set of figures can be consulted to learn what was spent for the current product. Since what was spent was used to buy the goods and services produced, these figures can be regarded as the money value of the national product.

Individual consumers spend money for food, clothing, rent, and a thousand other things. These expenditures can be added up by consulting the statistics of sales.

Business also spends money. In order to avoid duplication, we cannot count what it pays out for making the goods which consumers buy. That is all included in the item in the previous paragraph. What we must count is that part of business profits and borrowings which is spent directly by business itself for new investment in such things as buildings and machinery. For convenience's sake, all the new houses built are included in business spending, whether they are paid for by investors or by the individuals who live in them.

Some investment goes to foreign countries. It is convenient to make a separate item for foreign investment, since this can be checked by a separate group of figures about foreign trade and other international transactions.

The spending of individuals and business listed above does not include what these groups pay in taxes or lend to government by buying government bonds. It is better to regard government (federal, state, and local) as a sort of buying agency of the people, and to list separately what it pays out for the services of government employees and for goods.

There are, therefore, four main items of expenditure (or product): (1) those goods and services bought for personal consumption; (2) those goods which business bought for investment within this country; (3) investment abroad; and (4) those goods and services that government bought. These are the four great parts of the national product which together determine how large the product is, when measured by what is spent for it. It is convenient to list them separately in analyzing the total demand.

In 1961 the figures were as shown in Table 2.

Why is this total called "*gross* national product"? In the definitions previously quoted, the terms used have been "*net* income" or "*net* product."

The difference is that, in the figure here given for private investment in the United States, allowance is made for the wearing out or junking of old machinery or buildings during the year. In other words, there is an allowance for depreciation or obsolescence. Charges for these items are almost invariably made on their books by business concerns and are deducted before profits are reckoned, or any use of profits is made. Gross national product is therefore larger than net national income.

TABLE 2. GROSS NATIONAL PRODUCT (1961)
MEASURED BY EXPENDITURE

(Billions of Dollars)

Individuals spent for consumption	338.1
Total gross private investment in the U. S. was	69.3
Foreign trade and other transactions resulted in a net increase of foreign investments amounting to	4.0
Finally, the federal, state, and local governments bought goods and services for a total of	107.4
These various uses of money accounted for everything produced and sold for final use. This total is called *gross national product*	518.8

The figure for gross national product is useful in showing how much was actually spent or produced in a given year. Net product or net income is a better figure, however, to indicate how much the population received in "final products" during that year.

In order to change gross product to net product, it is necessary to make a deduction for depreciation which will show what "net investment" was. This deduction is called "capital consumption allowances." In 1961 it amounted to 45.3 billion dollars. If this figure be subtracted from the gross national product, there is left a total which is called the "net national product," amounting to 473.5 billion dollars. According to definition, income equals product. But even the figure called net national product is considerably larger than the figure for net national income. The difference is not a result of errors in counting, adding, or subtracting. It now becomes necessary to see what does explain it.

Double-Entry Check

Double-entry bookkeeping is familiar in every business. It means merely that every transaction is entered on both sides of the books. Thus, the money received for goods goes on one side, and the value of the goods sold on the other. The totals must balance if the books are accurately kept. A similar procedure now enables a check on national income accounting. Income received was totaled in the first table. From largely independent figures, we have listed how the money was spent, or otherwise disposed of. But still the books do not balance.

To discover where the discrepancy lies, it is necessary to check the figures for expenditure against the figures for income, to see whether there is any kind of spending listed for which no corresponding source of income is included.

First, personal expenditures for consumption come out of personal incomes, all listed in the first table. No discrepancy there.

Second, investment, both domestic and foreign, comes partly out of personal incomes and partly out of business profits, both accounted for in income received. Again no discrepancy.

Government spending for goods and services is paid for partly by taxes and borrowings which come out of personal incomes. All personal incomes are included in the first table. Government spending also is paid for in part by taxes and borrowings derived from business. Business *income* taxes and bond purchases come out of business profits, which are listed on the income table. But business also pays many other kinds of taxes—excise, property, tariff duties, etc., which are charged up to expenses. Business expenses are not included in the income table.

An allowance must be made, in our double-entry bookkeeping, for these *indirect* and other business taxes. In 1961 they amounted to 48.2 billion dollars.

Government interest payments have been excluded from both income and expenditure. So have "transfer payments"—that is, receipts and expenditures for social security and the like.

Two more minor technical corrections must be made, called "business transfer payments" and "subsidies minus current surplus of government enterprises." Then we arrive at comparable totals for income and for expenditures—or product, which is what the expenditures buy. There remains a difference of 3.1 billion dollars, which represents some unknown inaccuracy in the compilation of the figures, called "statistical discrepancy." It may be caused in part by the fact that many incomes are under-reported in income-tax returns, which are used in compiling the figures. This is a small error in so large a total—less than 1 per cent.

Another way of classifying income is by the source—that is, the industry or occupation from which it is derived, such as manufacturing industries, mining, construction, agriculture, trade, finance, government.

Many kinds of subdivision or cross-classification are possible, each with its own uses.

The relationship between national income, net national product, and gross national product is shown in Table 3. The figures are those for 1961.

TABLE 3. RELATION OF GROSS NATIONAL PRODUCT AND NATIONAL INCOME, 1961[1]

(Billions of Dollars)

Gross national product	518.8
Less capital consumption allowances	45.3
Net national product	473.5
Plus subsidies less current surplus of government enterprises	1.7
Less indirect business taxes	48.2
Less business transfer payments	2.1
Statistical discrepancy	—3.1
National income	427.8

[1] Compiled from Economic Report of the President, January 1963, p. 186, Table C-12.

Another important way of classifying national product, which cuts across this one, is that which distinguishes durable goods, nondurable goods, services, and construction. Automobiles, furniture, household equipment, are examples of durable goods. Food is classified as perishable.

There are also various subordinate accounts which show what happens in parts of the total picture. There is, for instance, a consolidated business account, which shows what business, if considered as a single concern, pays out and what it receives. The items in this table are almost the same as those for business in the national account.

There is, besides, a personal income account, which shows the total of individual incomes—this time including governmental interest—and on the other side, personal expenditures, tax payments, and savings. "Disposable income" excludes taxes, and so covers what people can either spend or save. The term is usually employed when discussing the effect of income on markets for consumers' goods, or the division of personal incomes between spending and saving.

Two other subsidiary accounts are separated out by the Department of Commerce. One is the government account (including, of course, federal, state, and local governments). The other is the foreign account. It is worth pausing a moment on the foreign account to see why, in our general table, only the net foreign investment (or its opposite, disinvestment) is included as a separate item in the list of spending.

The proceeds of foreign trade activity, in so far as they affect incomes, turn up in wages, salaries, profits, interest, or rent, listed on the income table. There is no need of a separate classification for them in our national income accounts. What Americans buy from abroad is automatically included in the various items of expenditures. We need include only the *difference* between incoming and outgoing payments. That difference must be an increase or decrease in debt, or in gifts or grants. The debt of the debtor is an investment of the creditor. There is no way other than by loans (or gifts) to finance an export surplus or an import surplus—unless payment is made in gold. By including net gold shipments in the figure for net foreign investment, we cover the whole matter.

It is necessary to add to the table this item for net foreign investment in order to balance the books, since what a country pays for imports in any one year almost never balances what it receives for exports.

Real National Income

The fact that the national income must be stated in money terms introduces distortions in comparing one year with another, since prices change, and dollars will buy more of the same goods and services at some times than at others. When no corrections are made for price changes in tables of the national income covering a series of years, there is usually a note that the totals are in terms of "current dollars." It is possible to correct for price changes, however, and this is usually done. When the correction has been made, and the yearly totals are still stated in the form of dollars, the note will state "1960 dollars" or "1929 dollars," or whatever year happens to be chosen as the basis of value. Income after correction for prices is usually spoken of as "real" income, whereas without correction for prices it is called "nominal" or "money" income. In our national accounts this tabulation of real income is stated in figures for Gross National Product—often spoken of by its nickname, "G. N. P."

A convenient way of showing changes over a period of time is by the use of index numbers. When this is done, the income of a certain year (or average of years) is given the number 100, and every other year in the series is expressed as a percentage of the base. Thus, if 1929 be chosen as the base, or 100, and income in some other year is 75 per cent of the base year, it will be represented by the number 75. Tables of index numbers usually carry a note indicating the base year, such as (Base—1929) or (1929=100).

From this brief review of some of the more important ways of reckoning or classifying figures of the national income, it will be seen that an enormous amount of information of many sorts may be derived from them. Because of the gaps in the raw data and the estimates which play a large part in the process, it is risky to place too much reliance on any exact accuracy in the figures, especially for the earlier years. Yet they do tell us much that is significant, as succeeding chapters will show.

THREE

THE NATIONAL INCOME AS HISTORY

The great mass of information accumulated in building up the totals called the national income can be used for dozens of different purposes. One of the most interesting is to learn what has happened to American economic fortunes in the past. Such facts also have a bearing on the present and the future. Some of them show trends which we hope will continue; some depict conditions which we may want to change, or misfortunes the repetition of which we should like to avoid.

Simon Kuznets, who did much of the pioneer work on the subject, provided a convenient summary up to World War II in his book *National Income, a Summary of Findings.* The figures he uses are not quite the same as those now published by the U. S. Department of Commerce, since the latter have embodied minor corrections and are based on slightly different definitions. These differences are not important for most purposes, however, and for the early years covered in this chapter—those up to 1929—Kuznets's figures are used.

It did not require study of the figures to tell Americans that there had been a remarkable increase in incomes since the Civil War. The figures, however, not only confirm this impression but add definiteness to it.

Per-Capita Income

To give meaning to such a demonstration, it is necessary to eliminate the effect of price fluctuations, since a given income could purchase more at some times than at others. This is done by stating the income for all years in dollars having the same purchasing power as in a given year—in the Kuznets figures, 1929. The yearly income of the population, if divided evenly, would have averaged $215 a person for the decade 1869 to 1878. In 1919 to 1928, it would have averaged $612, or almost three times as much as fifty years before. Bear in mind that this represents not just the dollars received, but what they could buy.

Increase of income does not necessarily mean an equivalent increase in welfare or in satisfaction in life. At the time of the Civil War, for instance, more of the people lived on farms and ate food that was raised on the farm instead of buying it. Homecooked food consumed on the farm does not appear in the income figures. The same is true of clothing made in the home in both city and country, and laundry or other work done without pay by the women of the household, a much larger proportion of whom now have paying jobs. Yet in so far as welfare depends on buying, people on the average have certainly grown more prosperous.

We turn now to figures from the Department of Commerce, beginning with 1929, which reveal the *disposable* income of persons. Dividing the total disposable income for each year by the population of that year, it finds the per-capita disposable income (in 1962 dollars). The per-capita disposable income so calculated had reached a peak, in 1929, of $1,240. Thereafter it declined for four years as the Great Depression of the 1930s chilled the economy like an advancing glacier. The low point was (in 1962 dollars) $913 in 1933. No such decline of real income can be found in any previous period in the history of the United States for which reliable records are available.

Recovery began in 1933, but real per-capita disposable income did not exceed the 1929 level until 1940—the year after World War II began. Thereafter it rose—with minor slumps in the postwar adjustment, and in 1954—to an estimated total of $2,051 in 1962, more than twice as much as in the worst years of depression and about $800 more than in 1929, the peak of prosperity in the 1920s.

Shifting Occupations

How was income apportioned among various important occupations? Here we find that marked changes have taken place. The share of agriculture has steadily declined. In the decade 1869 to 1878, agriculture had 27.5 per cent of the national income against only 10.5 per cent in the decade 1919 to 1928. During the same years the share of manufacturing increased from 17.1 per cent to 21.9 per cent, and mining increased from 1 per cent to 2.5 per cent. Construction was variable but had a smaller share of the national income at the end than at the beginning.

Many people assume that the relative shrinkage of agriculture was caused by a corresponding expansion of industry. The figures show that this was not wholly the case. While the share of manufacturing in the national income did increase, it did not grow nearly as rapidly as the share of agriculture fell. There had been a steady drop in the relative importance of commodity production taken as a whole. Those engaged in producing goods on farms, in factories, and in mines had 51.6 per cent of the national income in 1869 to 1878 and only 39.3 per cent in 1919 to 1928. The reason is an important advance in efficiency of production, which has made possible a great expansion in wholesale and retail trade, in finance, and in professional and other service occupations, such as teaching, automobile service, hairdressing, and so forth.

The shifts in shares of the national income which have occurred from decade to decade were accompanied by roughly corresponding changes in the number employed in each major occupation. After 1928 the number engaged in agriculture continued to fall off, not only relative to the total population but absolutely. The relative growth of manufacturing was temporarily checked immediately after World War I. From 1919 to 1928 its share of the total national income decreased slightly, while the number employed was about the same as in the preceding decade. In the thirties manufacturing employment had not only a relative but also an absolute decline. Manufacture, however, increased rapidly in World War II and since then has benefited from large defense expenditures by the government.

The fractions of national income originating in the major producing groups have shifted widely since 1929. (These shares include not only total wages and salaries but, in the case of private enterprise, rent, interest, and profits, both distributed and undistributed.)

The largest income producer in 1957—a fairly typical recent year—was manufacturing, with almost one-third of the total national income. It had risen from about one-fourth of the national income in 1929. Next in order was wholesale and retail trade, with more than one-sixth of the income in 1957; it had a slightly smaller share in 1929. Perhaps the most striking change was that in government enterprises, which accounted for one-eighth of the national income in

1957, having surged up from one-seventeenth in 1929. Services received more than one-tenth of the national income in 1957; their share had been slightly larger in 1929. Finance and insurance earned less than one-tenth of the national income in 1957—its share had dropped from one-seventh in 1929. (The deflation of speculative Wall Street in the great crash with which the 1920s ended accounted largely for this drop.)

Transportation's share fell from one-thirteenth in 1929 to one-twenty-first in 1957. (Much of its work has been transferred to private automobiles.) Contract construction rose from one-twentieth of the national income in 1929 to one-eighteenth in 1957. (It was doing fairly well in both years.) Communications and public utilities, though not important parts of the total income, increased their share from one-thirtieth in 1929 to one-twenty-seventh in 1957.

The most dramatic declines in the sources of income occurred, as before, in the extractive industries. Agriculture, forestry, and fisheries, in which originated between one-tenth and one-eleventh of the nation's income of 1929, fell to less than one-twenty-second of the income of 1957. Mining, which had accounted for one-forty-fourth of the 1929 income, contributed only one-fiftieth in 1957.

Some Groups Earn More than Others

We all know in a general way that average incomes in some industrial groups are higher than those in others. This has been true for many years. In the period between the world wars the per-capita income of workers in agriculture was just about half the per-capita income of workers in the nation as a whole. This does not count the food and housing which they received without paying for it. Per-capita income in mining and manufacturing was at the average level. The per-capita income of those engaged in trade was 10 per cent above the national average; in transportation and public utilities, it was 20 per cent above; in construction, it was 30 per cent above. At the top of the list stood finance and real estate, with 40 per cent above the average, and government employment, at the same figure. These figures refer to payments for work and do not include profits, rent, or interest. It is interesting to note, too, that the lowest per-capita returns were received by those who occupy a stage in production which is farthest from the ultimate consumer. Those engaged in primary production received less than those engaged in secondary production. These, in turn, received less than those engaged in transportation and distribution.

Inequalities of Distribution

One of the most striking recent changes in the economy of the United States is the approach toward equality of income which has taken place since the great panic of 1929. In 1929, the top 1 per cent of the recipients of income received 18.92 per cent of the total disposable personal income, whereas by 1946—the year after the end of World War II—they received only 7.71 per cent. The top 5 per cent of income receivers had in 1929 just over one-third of the disposable income—33.49 per cent; in 1946 they received about half as large a share—17.66 per cent. This change is not attributable mainly to high income-tax rates in the upper brackets; the figures reveal a consistent trend over the years, regardless of tax rates.

Perhaps a more meaningful tabulation of the change is one which shows the share of personal income received by purchasing units—families and unattached individuals. Table 4 indicates the changes, between 1929 and 1957, in share of income received by each fifth of these income receivers, from lowest to highest.

TABLE 4

	Percentage Share		
	1929	*1957*	
Lowest fifth	12.5	4.8	16.1
Second fifth		11.3	
Third fifth	13.8	16.3	
Fourth fifth	19.3	22.3	
Highest fifth	54.4	45.3	

The lowest plus the second-lowest fifth (which were not listed separately in 1929) received 12.5 per cent of the income in 1929, and 16.1 per cent in 1957—a gain of almost one-third. The share of the third fifth rose during the period from 13.8 per cent to 16.3 per cent—a somewhat smaller but marked percentage gain. Income of the fourth fifth increased from 19.3 per cent to 22.3 per cent, while the share of the highest fifth was reduced from 54.4 per cent to 45.3 per cent.

Absolute equality would, of course, mean that each fifth had 20 per cent of the income. The distribution of family income is still far from equal, of course, and is not likely ever to reach equality, but the trend over the past thirty-five years has been rapidly approaching it.

Meanwhile there has been a gain in the average real income of all the families and the individual consumer units. After paying federal income taxes, and in constant (1950) dollars, this average (mean) income increased from $3,339 in 1929 to $4,772 in 1957. Thus there has been not only an approach toward equality but a faster gain in the total amount of income to be divided than in the number of recipients. The gain is in real income (purchasing power), not just in the number of dollars and cents. In 1957 (as in later years as well) American families, on the average, could buy at least 40 per cent more with their incomes (after paying federal income tax) than in 1929, the year which marked the glittering but tragic peak of "Coolidge prosperity." The reduction of inequality occurred because the lower incomes gained more from the general increase than did the higher. For example, between 1941 and 1959, the lowest fifth had a gain in real income of 67 per cent, the second lowest a gain of 71 per cent, and the highest fifth a gain of 40 per cent.

In spite of the approach toward equality of income distribution, there is no ground for complacency. For example, most low-income families can manage to save little or nothing, either for a rainy day or as a source of income. The spending units earning less than $1,000 held only 3 per cent of the liquid assets in the nation in 1959, though they comprised 7 per cent of the spenders. Each thousand-dollar income bracket between $1,000 and $4,000 had only 6 per cent of the American people's liquid assets, though each of these groups comprised 10 to 12 per cent of the spenders. At the higher end of the income scale, those receiving from $5,000 to $7,499 comprised 26 per cent of the spending units and owned 23 per cent of the liquid assets, while those with $7,500 or above, who comprised 22 per cent of all spending units, owned 47 per cent of the liquid assets. Therefore, in a recent year, nearly seven-tenths of the nation's liquid assets belonged to the upper half of income receivers. (Liquid assets in this calculation consist of United States savings bonds, checking accounts, savings accounts in banks, shares in savings and loan associations and credit unions. Currency is not included.)

Other well-known disparities appear in the government figures—principally the fact that, on the average, white families and individuals received about twice as much as nonwhites (at least up to 1960), and that the median (middle between highest and lowest) income of rural farm families was about half that of urban and rural nonfarm families. There are, however, some farm families that do very well; in 1959, 36 per cent of the farm families received incomes of $6,000 or more, and 10.3 per cent had incomes of $10,000 or more.

Inequalities in distribution of income might conceivably be abolished by a rigid governmental control which would forcibly take from the higher brackets enough to bring the lower brackets up to equality. But in that case nobody would have very much. Increase in the national income as a whole faster than the increase in population has enabled distribution of a larger share to the poorer, with no absolute sacrifice by the richer. Gains in productivity—and this means of those in the lower brackets as well as of those in the upper—constitute what is perhaps the best method by which to remedy undesirable inequality. A policy of encouraging enlargement of output per person or per man-hour may readily be combined with social insurance and minimum standards which set a floor below which no income may be allowed to fall.

The figures here cited do not prove that such measures as raising money wages, social insurance, and minimum hourly rates of pay are responsible for growth in total income by broadening mass markets. Neither do they prove that growth in national productivity has automatically brought with it a less unequal distribution. They show merely that both outcomes are compatible, and establish a strong probability that further gains in both output per capita and approach toward equality of distribution may be achieved.

Where Incomes Come From

As would be expected, the lower-income groups receive most of their compensation as employees or for services rendered, whereas the upper-income groups derive more from dividends or property income. In the inter-war period 69.7 per cent of the dividends went to the upper 1 per cent of the individuals receiving incomes. Rent and interest are somewhat more equally divided, but not wholly so. Taking the national income as a whole, and classifying it according to the various types of payment, we find that 84.2 per cent was paid for work performed, in the form of wages, salaries, or earnings of working owners such as farmers, while the other 15.8 per cent was paid as a return on property. Further subdivision shows that 66 per cent of the total national income consisted of employee compensation, 18.2 per cent went to individual businessmen and farmers, 5.9 per cent was paid in dividends, 6.9 per cent in interest, and 3 per cent in rent.

A more recent estimate shows, as might be expected, that in 1960 the spending units in the lower-income brackets owned a smaller percentage of corporate stock than those in the upper brackets. Fifty-six per cent of those in the highest income bracket—$15,000 and over—owned stock, and of these almost half owned stock worth $10,000 and more. The percentage owning stock, and the value of their holdings, shrink rapidly, the lower the income: of those in the lowest bracket (under $3,000) only 5 per cent owned stock and only 1 per cent owned stock worth $10,000 or more. "The public" often referred to in discussion of the stock market is really only a small fraction of the population.

What Consumers Bought

Many other important and interesting facts are known about the distribution of income, such as the differences among regions and the differences among cities of various sizes, rural and farm localities. But let us pass on to a few things that the figures tell us about purchases by consumers. In the inter-war period consumers spent about 40 per cent of their budgets for perishable goods such as food, about 15 per cent for semi-durable goods such as clothing, slightly less than 10 per cent for durable goods such as automobiles and furniture, and 36 per cent for services. The chief change during the period was that a smaller proportion was spent for perishable goods and a larger proportion for durable goods and for services. This trend has continued.

It is a very important fact that, as incomes grow, people spend a larger and larger proportion for things like automobiles, electric refrigerators, and furniture. These things can be made to last longer than clothing or nondurables such as kitchen supplies. Their purchase is more largely financed by credit. Therefore the demand for them may vary widely from one year to another—much more widely than the demand for food or even clothing. This means that, as they assume a more prominent role in the economic picture, the instability of the whole order, and of the employment and income which it supplies, may be greatly increased. A falling off in production of motorcars, for instance, can easily occur and can have serious consequences.

Saving and Investment

Between 1919 and 1939 about 6 per cent of the national income was saved and invested in new capital facilities. This proportion of saving to total income seems surprisingly small when we consider the immense increase in production and productive efficiency which occurred in the 1920s. We must remember, however, that during the thirties, especially while depression was rampant, new investment was small, and in some of these years net capital formation was a negative quantity.

Since World War II, two developments in saving and investment have been noteworthy. One is that business has financed out of its own saved profits—those not distributed in dividends to stockholders—a large part of its new investment in plant and equipment. Such surpluses are commonly called "retained earnings." For example, in 1960 American business invested in the United States a total of 72.8 billion dollars, of which only 20.8 billion dollars came from personal and other sources of savings; 52 billion dollars was derived from the retained earnings of business concerns themselves.

The other development is the enlarged stimulus to the national economy from spending by federal, state, and local governments. When governments are spending more than they collect, they stimulate economic activity. If, in consequence, demand should increase faster than the available supplies at existing prices, the result would be a rise in prices (inflation) rather than increase in goods and services, but this need not be the outcome in an economy which has unused labor and other resources. Of the ten years 1951-1960 there were six in which federal, state, and local government had deficits as measured in the income and product account. The largest such deficit was 11.4 billion dollars in 1958; the total deficit for the six years was 31.9 billion dollars.

Losses from Depression

The national income figures also tell us a great deal about the huge losses incurred by the nation because of depressions.

In the two decades between the wars there were five years which showed large declines in the national income and three others in which the increase was negligible. The same is true of employment. The average drop in income for each depression year was 4 per cent of the average yearly income for the whole period. The loss occasioned by depression is still more dramatically shown by another type of calculation. Kuznets has calculated what the national income might reasonably have been expected to be during the inter-war period if it had continued at the level of full capacity. This estimate is a conservative one, since it assumes that the production achieved at the top of prosperity was somewhat larger than could have been steadily maintained. On this basis, he finds that the income might have been more than 13 per cent greater for the twenty years than it actually was. Remember that this calculation includes not only the depressed thirties but the prosperous twenties.

During the Great Depression of the 1930s, total income payments to individuals dropped almost half—by 45 per cent. A study of family incomes made by a sampling method shows an average fall of 37 per cent between 1929 and 1933.

The depression also had curious effects on the distribution of income. Inequality was, on the whole, increased. The gulf between the lower and the upper groups of income was widened. Within the lower 50 to 70 per cent of incomes, there was also more inequality. This is probably accounted for by the fact that the millions of unemployed received comparatively little, while those who held their jobs were not much worse off than before.

Within the upper-income groups which received a larger share of the total income during the depression, there was less inequality than usual, although the very topmost incomes declined relative to the others. These high incomes are derived largely from profits, which fall drastically during depression.

Conclusions for Policy

What broad conclusions are we justified in drawing from the facts here summarized? First, while it would be socially desirable to reduce the extreme inequality in the distribution of income, any progress in this direction would not help much to alleviate poverty without large increases in the total product of the nation. This conclusion is reinforced by the experience of inflation after the Second World War. Though in 1947 almost everybody was employed, and the total output of the nation was about half again as large as before the war, there still were not nearly enough goods to satisfy the demands of the population. When people have plenty of money to spend, it becomes more apparent that not enough is produced, even yet.

Second, there will be plenty of opportunity to sell to consumers all the extra goods that might be produced if we can distribute to those at the lower end of the income scale sufficient money to buy them. It is obvious that the families who have incomes of less than $2,000 must have many unsatisfied wants. We are nowhere near the saturation point of people's desire for goods and services.

Clearly the principal economic objective must be to increase the production and distribution of needed goods and services. That this objective is attainable is indicated by the fact that there has been a marked tendency to increase over a long period of years. Whether that increase has been greater or less than it might have been under some other form of economic organization, these figures do not indicate.

Finally, the most important obstacle to the desired increase which the figures do show is the frequent recurrence of depression and unemployment. Avoiding depression, therefore, is a most important objective.

There is nothing startling about these conclusions, which are probably accepted by the majority of Americans today. It is worth remembering, however, that they were not nearly so generally accepted within the memory of many living men. The experience of the Great Depression, of course, had much to do with the change in the mental climate, but the advance in economic science, which is marked by the study of the national income and which dates from the end of World War I, has given us the solid documentation which has established the character of our situation beyond dispute.

FOUR

UPS AND DOWNS OF BUSINESS

Nothing reveals the myopia of classical economic theory for the facts of life more clearly than that its system of thought allowed no place for industrial depressions. One would think that men who set out to explain economic phenomena would study the oscillations of production and employment almost before they noticed anything else. What early theorists did, on the contrary, was to conclude that the natural forces of the economic order would keep it in balance at a high level of employment. There could, they believed, be no such thing as a general shortage of demand in a private-enterprise economy with free markets.

Later theorists of the classical school could not deny that unemployment did occur or that business conditions were sometimes bad. These inconvenient facts did not, however, induce them to alter the fundamentals of their thought. They found two kinds of excuses for the wide difference between the actual behavior of the world and the manner in which their theory said it ought to behave. One was that something from outside the economic order intervened and set it wobbling. For instance, Stanley Jevons suggested that business fluctuations arose from variations in the farmers' income, that these in turn depended on weather, and that there was a weather cycle arising from sunspots. This was a pretty reasonable guess, as guesses go. There is indeed a weather cycle. Yet there does not seem to be any regular relation between the farmers' fortunes and the oscillation of business conditions.

The other road of escape which the classical theorists found was to admit (and usually to deplore) that people did not act according to the premises on which their theory was built. Monopolies or partial monopolies interfered with perfect competition. Capital did not flow easily from one use to another; labor would not readily shift jobs. Prices, instead of responding promptly to changes in demand and supply, were "sticky." These frictions and rigidities delayed the automatic readjustment in the direction of wholesome equilibrium which the theoretical system expected.

There was nothing wrong with these observations; such rigidities and frictions do indeed exist. What was wrong was the fact that many followers of the theory stuck to their premises and attempted to brush away the facts as something extraordinary, outside the "natural" order. The result was that their only remedy was to exhort people to comply with the "natural" law. This is shown no more clearly than in the classical analysis of unemployment. According to the doctrine, employers would always hire everybody seeking work if only wages were low enough. Falling prices were supposed to stimulate demand; falling wages would therefore stimulate the demand for labor. The cause of unemployment was thus found in the refusal of workers to accept low enough wages. This reasoning led to the strange conclusion that unemployment was the fault of the unemployed; there was no such thing as involuntary unemployment. This reasoning did *not* lead to any scientific discoveries about depressions.

As more attention began to be paid to the problem, a host of explanations was offered for the persistent rhythms of business activity. It would require a long book to summarize the many varieties of business-cycle theory. But such a book would be more confusing than enlightening, since most of the explanations advanced have been based on guesses, partial observations, emphasis on one or two factors which overlooked the rest. Many of the theories are mutually inconsistent; some of the better ones fit some of the facts, but none fits all of them.

Scientific Exploration of the Cycle

At last a serious effort was made to accumulate and analyze all the facts available. Ever since the 1920s the National Bureau of Economic Research, with a competent staff of economists and statisticians, has been studying the data under the direction of the chief American authority on the subject, Wesley C. Mitchell, and his successors, notably Arthur F. Burns, Solomon Fabricant, and Geoffrey Moore. They accumulated and carefully analyzed mountainous piles of statistics going back for about a century, and for four nations—the United States, Britain, France, and Germany. They established the historical turning points, or "reference dates," and then studied the behavior of some eight hundred statistical series in every cycle, having corrected the figures to eliminate seasonal influences. Of these series, 13 covered general business activity, 135 had to do with finance, 168 indicated change in prices, and 148 showed the flow of commodities, services, and income. The first object was not to prove or disprove any preconceived theory, or even, as yet, to test any hypothesis at all. They wanted to see first what the business cycle looks like in reality, and how economic processes actually behave. Once the facts are properly arranged, it becomes easier to formulate appropriate theories and to test them.

One of the first jobs in an effort of this kind was to make a rough definition of just what was the subject under observation. According to Dr. Mitchell's definition, a business cycle is a fluctuation of the aggregate economic activity of a nation; it consists of expansions occurring at about the same time in many lines, followed by contractions. The contractions, in turn, are followed by revivals, which merge into the expansion of the next cycle.

Though there are periods of relative quiet, there never has been a flat calm in the recorded history of any business-enterprise economy. There are longer periods of expansion or contraction, but the business cycle is defined as a relatively short up-and-down movement, ranging from more than a year to, occasionally, ten or twelve years. It is described as "recurrent but not periodic." This means that although it is continually repeated, like the seasons of the year, it is unlike the seasons in that there is no fixed interval between booms or depressions. Some cycles are short and others are long; some are extreme in their rises and falls, others are moderate. Cycles of different duration or amplitude do not follow one another in any regular order. What we do know is that, if history is repeated, there will surely be an expansion after a contraction and a contraction after an expansion.

The Method of Measurement

Great care was devoted to devising a method of measurement that would not conceal any assumptions which might need testing against the facts discovered. One favorite method, still prevalent in discussions of the subject, is to assume that there is a long-term trend of business activity which is independent of the shorter fluctuations, and that the business cycle consists of dips below this trend and bulges above it. Use of this method involves charting a trend line and then measuring against it the shorter waves of the business curve.

Tracing the cycle against a trend is unsatisfactory because the measurements of the cycle differ according to how the trend line is placed, and that depends on a rather arbitrary judgment. Instead, the bureau found a way of measuring, charting, and studying each successive cycle without placing it on a trend. This involved no assumption as to what part of a given upward movement, for instance, must be attributed to long-term expansion and what part to cyclical forces. The method was quite clear as to when the top was reached and when the ensuing decline ended. It showed what happened in between and permitted a comparison of one cycle with any other.

Measured in this way, there were thirty-one complete business cycles in the United States between 1836 and 1961. Between 1854 and 1885, the average cycle lasted about five years; since 1885, it has lasted nearly four. But it would not do to apply this conclusion too literally. This average length covers wide differences. The variation of the length of the cycle within each period is much greater than the variation between the average of the first period and that of later ones. Between 1854 and 1885 the shortest cycle lasted thirty months and the longest one ninety-nine months. In the more recent period the shortest cycle lasted twenty-eight months and the longest eighty-eight. Anyone who attempted to forecast the next boom on the basis of the average length of the cycle would be putting his money on a long shot.

Important and illuminating conclusions did, however, result from the continued study. Among these are:

About 90 per cent of the statistical series on various economic processes vary with some relationship to the business cycle; the rest appear independent of it. Those that do change in the course of a cycle are subject to wide variation in the extent to which they conform with the cycle as a whole.

The series that do change with the general movement of the economy differ in the times of their turning points.

At *every* phase of the cycle, some statistical series are going down and others are going up. Recession is characterized by a bunching of downward activities, recovery by a bunching of upward indexes. In the next chapter we shall see what use may be made of this phenomenon in attempts to forecast the economic weather.

Are Depressions Getting Worse?

Karl Marx predicted that the commercial crises which always accompany capitalism would become worse as time goes on. Many, after the disastrous experience of the 1930s, agreed with him. The researchers, looking back over the experience of a hundred years, can find no such trend. It is true that the slump beginning in 1929 was unusually severe and unusually long, but there were bad ones in earlier parts of the period studied, in the 1870s and 1880s, for example. And there have been some relatively short or mild ones in recent years. The bureau's judgment on this point is not a mere impression; it is based on the most rigorous and careful statistical analysis.

Lest anyone become too optimistic, however, it is necessary to record the twin judgment that there is no proof of the theory, widely held in the 1920s and being revived today, that depressions will get milder as time goes on. Dr. Mitchell found no factual support for any long-term trend, either for the worse or for the better.

The only change which appears in the statistics—and this is of doubtful validity when the experience of other countries is considered—is an apparent reduction of the average duration of the cycle.

Facts about the Cycle

The National Bureau has discovered a multitude of interesting facts about the business cycle, some of which have already been published and more of which will be revealed and discussed in its future volumes. A good many of these facts have a bearing on various theories in the field. Some previous hunches have been corroborated, others have been disproved. Most of these discoveries are too technical to be described in a short treatment of the subject.

My own guess is that the bureau will never emerge from the statistical depths, like a pearl diver, bearing aloft that priceless jewel, *the* cause of depressions. It is not likely to say, for instance, that they are caused by overproduction, or underconsumption, or oversaving, or disparity between investment and the propensity to consume. What it will do, rather, is to show in multitudinous detail what the process of business fluctuation is like and what the relative magnitudes of important factors are. It is likely to cast light on the critical points where intervention might have a desirable effect.

Among the interesting facts made plain—some of which have been observed before, but not with such precision or in the setting of so thorough a view of the whole subject—are the following:

Business cycles affect both prices and volume of production. By and large, they affect any specific industry or occupation by a reciprocal combination of these two. That is, if the price fall of any article is great during a depression, there will be less fall in the volume of its production, and vice versa. Thus, the output of agricultural commodities typically is not much affected by a slump, but the prices of these commodities fall drastically. On the other hand, the output of steel drops far during depression, while the price is much less affected.

Some parts of the economy are relatively little affected by the swings of the business cycle, through either change in price or change in output. Services directly rendered to consumers, such as telephone or electrical utilities, are in this category. Indeed, in these two cases, as in a number of others, the fact that rates are under public control prevents rapid change in prices. The large and growing governmental sector of the economy does not normally lay off employees or trim its other expenditures when recession arrives. Post-office employees, teachers in public schools, and many others working for governments need have no fear of unemployment arising from depression—except in a calamity like that of the 1930s.

That part of investment which consists of business inventories conforms very sensitively to the swings of the cycle. Its fluctuations accounted for about half the difference in the flow of gross investment between the top of prosperity and the bottom of depression during the years between World War I and World War II. Indeed, they were so great as to account for more than one-fifth of the cyclical changes in the gross national product.

In general, private investment shows wide swings during cycles. Between 1919 and 1935, out of every $100 of gross national product, $80.80 was spent for consumers' goods and $19.20 on investment (including replacement of existing capital). Among the goods consumers buy, their purchases of durable goods, such as automobiles and furniture, show the widest swings. Consumers paid for these $9.50 of their $80.80 of spendings. Combining the gross investment (which swings widely) and the purchase of durable consumer goods (which swings widely), we get $28.70 out of $100, or 29 per cent of the gross national product. We should have the cycle nearly licked if we could stabilize this large fraction of the nation's spending (though of course we should have to be careful, in doing so, not to produce undesirable results of another kind).

Are There Other Kinds of Cycles?

There are cycles in specific types of activity which differ in length and timing from the general business cycle. For instance, in agriculture there is a well-defined cycle in the production of hogs, which depends upon the relationship between the price of pork products and the price of corn. There is another cycle in the production of livestock, which has something to do with the time necessary to breed and increase herds and the oversupply that usually follows. There is a very well-defined cycle in building construction which affects many related industries. Its course from peak to peak is around fifteen to twenty years.

Recently Simon Kuznets, Moses Abramowitz, and others, most of whom have been associated with the National Bureau of Economic Research and make use of statistical studies, have conducted inquiries into the possibility of "long swings" in the economy as a whole, which, if they exist, as the evidence seems to show, occupy about twenty years in their upward and downward movements together. They are measured by their deviation from the average yearly growth of the real gross national product over a period of nearly a century. Thus the downward phase of the long swing does not necessarily indicate that the output of the nation is declining, but may mean merely that it is growing more slowly than during the upward phase of the long swing. It is true, however, that in the past the troughs of these long swings usually occurred during unusually severe depressions.

Attempts to discover whether the long swings are connected with important recurring forces in the economy or, on the other hand, are haphazard, have revealed long cyclical variations in population growth, in immigration (before it was drastically limited in the early 1920s), in the size of the labor force, in the construction cycle, and in investment of the type due to new inventions or other technological advance. Any one of these forces might have influenced the others; it is difficult, to say the least, to prove that any one of them was *the* cause of long swings and others were the consequences. For example, a gain in population may have stimulated house building, which in turn led to more investment on the part of suppliers of materials and of real-estate interests; these developments could have brought larger employment and increased wages, the spending of which could have stimulated retail markets. Yet it is just as logical to observe that an increase in the birth rate and a rise in immigration—both of which may contribute to growth of population—may have been the result of enlargement of investment, or of employment, or of rising wages.

Apparently it is important—but difficult—to discover what triggers the upward and downward phases of the long cycle. In this connection an early hypothesis stated by Wesley Mitchell should not be forgotten: "After a severe depression industrial activity rebounds sharply, but speculation does not. The following contraction in business is mild, which leads people to be less cautious. Consequently, in the next two or three [business or short] cycles, while the cyclical advances become progressively smaller in industrial activity, they become progressively larger in speculative activity. Finally, the speculative boom collapses and a drastic liquidation follows, which ends this cycle of cycles and brings us back to our starting point." The experience of the 1920s, as well as the collapse of speculative booms in the more remote past, suggests that this observation may be important.

But this hypothesis is advanced only for further study; no simple pattern applies invariably.

The study does substantiate the belief that when the long-term trend of prices is downward, the contraction phase of the business cycle is longer, and vice versa.

FIVE

EXPERIMENTS IN FORECASTING

The economic soothsayers who flourished in the 1920s resembled amateur athletes riding surfboards dangerously on the rolling breakers of stock-market speculation. The 1929 tidal wave, crashing on the beach, was unforeseen by most of the oracles and left behind it a bitter but healthy distrust of forecasters. Even those few who happened to make good predictions usually did so on the basis of the wrong reasons.

During the 1920s, on the other hand, the economic scientists who were analyzing the business cycle in detail never issued a "dope sheet" or published a forecast. Their painstaking work in statistical laboratories continued during the turmoil of the 1930s and the ensuing partial recovery. At length they contributed tentative findings, which might be of use in plotting the location of the ship of state on the economic tides.

On May 28, 1938, the National Bureau of Economic Research published Bulletin 69, by Wesley C. Mitchell and Arthur F. Burns, entitled *Statistical Indicators of Cyclical Revivals*. It was originally prepared as a memorandum "at the request of a public agency" which wanted to know whether a revival from the recession of 1938 was in prospect, and when it might be expected.

This report defined the desirable qualities of "an ideal statistical indicator." There is, in fact, none which conforms perfectly with their prescriptions. "It is because of the past shortcomings of the most trustworthy indicators we have been able to find that we think it unsafe to base judgments of current conditions on the behavior of any one series, or of a few series. The likelihood of being misled is reduced, though not eliminated, if one uses a considerable number of series, each with a good past record as an indicator, and representing in the aggregate a wide range of business activities."

The authors of the report analyzed 487 statistical series in the United States and picked out 71 as "tolerably consistent in the behavior of their timing in relation to business cycle revivals"—and "also of cyclical recessions." Some rather consistently led the general cycle, some were nearly coincidental, and some lagged behind. The average lead or lag of each series was tabulated, and erratic movements of each were assessed. The amplitude of each of these "specific cycles"—that is, cycles of any one indicator, such as orders for structural steel, factory payrolls, business failures, etc.—was compared with that of the general business cycle. From the 71 "tolerably consistent" specific series the authors picked 21 as the "most trustworthy." The bulletin ends with several pages discussing necessary cautions and unavoidable difficulties in forecasting, even on the basis of the most carefully chosen list of indicators. Among these are:

It is difficult to discount seasonal variations in series which often behave differently in these variations from year to year.

There are erratic fluctuations in specific series, not significant with regard to the business cycle. For example, a drop in the stock market may soon be wiped out by a rise; it is difficult to measure a trend until after it has occurred.

The cyclical behavior of indicators varies even from cycle to cycle. The sequence of turning points for some specific series may change.

So far, attempts to combine indicators into a single index, which might be applied to forecasting, had not been successful. Five general indexes of "business activity" were included among the 487 series analyzed by the authors; of these only one was qualified for their short list, and that had average leads of only two months.

The next time the reader finds on the business or financial page of his newspaper an airy note by some commentator that because of the recent rise of a single "indicator" the confidence of the market traders had been bolstered, he may well be wary. He should note the final paragraph of the Mitchell and Burns Bulletin 69:

> So far as we know, there is no certain way of telling at the time it begins whether an incipient revival will suffer a relapse or develop into a cyclical expansion. Yet the occasions are frequent when speculation about the future course of business is

demanded by pressing present needs. Those whose hard duty it is to make these guesses have the best chance of being substantially right if they combine analysis of current data with some knowledge of the history of business cycles, such information as is available concerning important factors outside the realm of business, and a firm determination not to let their hopes and fears color their judgments more than is inevitable.

A Postwar Experiment

After World War II, Geoffrey Moore of the National Bureau undertook an experiment—to discover how the twenty-one best indicators picked by Mitchell and Burns in 1938 had behaved in subsequent cycles. His conclusions were published in 1950, with the title *Statistical Indicators of Cyclical Revivals and Recessions*. The reader will note that this study included the attempt to forecast recessions as well as revivals, by observation of the whole range of indicators chosen—leading series, coincident series, and lagging series. Moore discovered that although many of the twenty-one indicators previously selected were still useful, some changes had to be made. On the whole, however, the original list of twenty-one indicators stood up fairly well in cycles which took place after they were first chosen by Mitchell and Burns.

Nevertheless, the experts in the subject were not yet satisfied that improvements could not be made. By 1958 three complete cycles after World War II had been experienced—1946-1949, 1949-1954, and 1954-1958—and they suggested some revision, although the record of the original twenty-one indicators was still good. Moore noted that in these three postwar business cycles there had been one hundred and twenty upturns and downturns in the specific cycles of the indicators, and that, of these turns, 70 per cent "occurred where expected relative to business cycle turns." The "errors" were smaller than the "successes," not only in number but in average magnitude. If one looked at the whole picture rather than at the behavior of one or a few indicators, the point at which the economy probably stood in the business cycle at any given time was fairly clear. The need was to make it still clearer by use of new information, discovered since the 1950 list of indicators was chosen.

Moore therefore selected in 1960 twenty-six indicators, of which twelve are classified as leading the general business cycle, nine as roughly coincident with it, and five as lagging. "Fifteen of the twenty-six are on the 1950 list. Five more are substitutes for closely related series"—for example, a series on housing starts was substituted for residential building contracts. "One indicator on the 1950 list has been dropped: freight car-loadings," because the railroads now carried a much diminished share of the nation's freight. Three series were reclassified: personal income and retail sales were shifted from the lagging to the roughly coincident group, and corporate profits from the coincident to the leading group.

Many of the changes from the original 1937 list of twenty-one indicators resulted from new and more significant statistical series covering the same activities. Other changes add activities in which monthly or quarterly data were not available until recent years. As the record stood in 1960, the best indicators were as follows:

A. Twelve Leading Indicators

Sensitive employment and unemployment indicators

1. Average work week in manufacturing (hours)
2. Accession rate in manufacturing (per 100 employees)
3. Lay-off rate in manufacturing, inverted (per 100 employees)

New investment commitments

4. New orders for durable goods (billion $)
5. Housing starts (millions)
6. Commercial and industrial building contracts (floor space, mil. sq. ft.)
7. Change in number of businesses (thousands)

Profits, business failures, and stock prices

8. Liabilities of business failures, inverted (million $)
9. Corporate profits (billion $, annual rate)
10. Index of stock prices (1941-1943=100)

Inventory investment and sensitive commodity prices

11. Change in business inventories (billion $)
12. Industrial raw materials price index (1947-1949=100)

B. Nine Roughly Coincident Indicators

Employment and unemployment

13. Employment in nonagricultural establishments (millions)
14. Unemployment rate, inverted (per cent)

Production

15. Industrial Production Index, including utilities (1947-1949=100)
16. Gross National Product in current dollars (billion $, annual rate)
17. Gross National Product in 1954 dollars (billion $, annual rate)

Income and trade

18. Bank debits outside New York City (billion $)
19. Personal income (billion $, annual rate)
20. Retail sales (billion $)

Wholesale prices

21. Wholesale price index, excluding farm products and food (1947-1949=100)

C. Five Lagging Indicators

22. Plant and equipment expenditures (billion $)
23. Wage and salary cost per unit of output, manufacturing (million $ per index point)
24. Manufacturers' inventories (billion $)
25. Consumer installment debt (billion $)
26. Bank interest rate, business loans (per cent)

These indicators were chosen by observation of what had actually happened during the ups and downs of the economy; they are not principles deduced from a comprehensive theory, but are, as scientists would say, an example of inductive or empirical discovery. Nevertheless they do make logical sense when interpreted as a rough analysis of the business cycle and correspond rather closely with Wesley Mitchell's posthumous work (edited by Arthur F. Burns) *What Happens during Business Cycles,* published in 1950.

Let us suppose the economy is experiencing a recession, and we wish to spot any signs of improvement in business conditions. Naturally, we look at indicators which have led the procession in the past. The first three of the leading indicators in the preceding list have to do with employment. We find that (1) in manufacturing establishments the average work week (measured by hours) is expanding. During the slump it may have been shortened; certainly fewer establishments would have worked overtime. We also find that (2) manufacturers are, on the average, rehiring employees at a faster rate and also beginning to hire new workers, while

(3) they are not laying off employees so freely as before. All this seems to indicate that producers have new orders, or that their inventories of finished goods are getting low, or that they foresee more active sales. And the consequence of the upturn in employment will be that more workers have more money to spend.

Next, we look to see what is happening to investment in capital goods; an expansion of investment would surely be a favorable sign. We find that (4) the orders for durable goods have increased. Durable goods include machinery and equipment ordered by producers, and automobiles, furniture, household equipment and the like for sale to consumers. We also find that (5) more houses are being built, and (6) that contracts have been signed for more square feet of floor space in industrial and office buildings. And (7) the number of businesses has increased. More people are going into business than are going out of it. Business obviously is deciding to spend more than in the recent past.

The next group of leading indicators has to do with the financial situation of business. We see (8) that the total liabilities of business failures have been decreasing. The sum of corporate profits (9) is rising, and the reflection of these and other favorable changes (10) is seen in a rising index of stock prices.

Finally, among the leading indicators, we see that business is increasing its inventories (11) (by buying more materials and enlarging its volume of work in progress and of finished goods for sale). These facts are eloquent testimony that businessmen expect better times and are making commitments to spend more money.

We can make the same kind of common-sense interpretations that fit the leading indicators in the cases of the other two main groups—coincident indicators and lagging indicators.

In looking at the coincident indicators under group B, it could scarcely surprise anyone to discover that at a peak of the business cycle, employment (13) is high and unemployment (14) low, that the physical index of industrial production (15) is at the top, and that the gross national product (16 and 17) is high. The activity of banking operations (18) outside of New York City, where they might be influenced by the speculative markets, would indicate humming business conditions. Surely both personal income (19) and retail sales (20) would be up, and wholesale prices (21) would also reflect prosperity.

Perhaps somewhat less obvious is the interpretation of the five indicators in Group C that lag behind the general cycle. Plant and equipment expenditures (22) may be at their largest after the general business cycle has passed its peak and turned downward, because of a lag between decisions to enlarge capacity and the actual construction and installation. There is also, possibly, overoptimism during a boom, which in turn can help to precipitate a downward trend in signing construction contracts, while previous contracts are still being fulfilled. The wage cost per unit of output (23) may be increased by wage gains greater than increase of productivity, after the top of prosperity has been passed. Thus unit profits may be decreased and incentive to enlarge output diminished. Increase of manufacturers' inventories (24) resulting from large orders for materials and piling up of the stock of goods in process and of finished goods is likely to appear as sales slacken. Consumers' installment debt (25) may easily be at its highest point after business has begun to feel the fall of profits, since consumer incomes as a whole are not affected so quickly or so much by an incipient recession as the incomes of business concerns. In so far as consumer income does shrink, installment obligations may grow merely by accumulation of unpaid installments.

In the preceding paragraphs we have traced possible explanations of the behavior of the twenty-six indicators—leading, coincident, and lagging—during recovery, peak and downward turn of the general business cycle. It would be equally possible to follow them through the contraction, low point, and upturn.

Diffusion Indexes

Any of the indicators may be subject to aberrations; there are random influences as well as those attributed to the general cycle. The general cycle itself occurs because of the bunching of upward or downward movements in a large number of component activities. In order to find a check on the possible vagaries of a relatively few indicators and to measure this bunching phenomenon, the "diffusion index" was devised.

In any phase of the cycle the individual series in any one group of indicators—leading, coincident, or lagging—are expected to move broadly in the same direction; but in fact they do not move simultaneously. Of the leading indicators, let us suppose that half are rising in one month, and half are falling. The diffusion index of this group would then show that 50 per cent are rising. One could not say that as a group the leading indicators were rising or falling. And let us suppose that in the following month 60 per cent rise. That would reveal an incipient rising tendency in the leading group of indicators as a whole. The diffusion index consists of a series of numbers which record the percentage which is rising, and thus helps in discounting any random or noncyclical movements within a group of specific indicators.

Not only may diffusion indexes be calculated for any particular group of specific indexes, such as the leading group, the roughly coincidental, or the lagging, but a diffusion index may cover the groups of indicators for all phases of the cycle. Moore computed such an index of the twenty-one indicators in his earlier list, for the three business cycles which occurred between 1948 and 1959. This index corresponds closely with the course of the three cycles which occurred during that period. It displays a tendency, which has been observed repeatedly in many cycles and is successful in forecasting, to recede from its highest level well before business activity reaches its peak. This reflects the fact that when business as a whole is most prosperous the number of activities sharing recessive tendencies will already have become large.

Forecasting the Severity of a Recession

Another experiment in forecasting was a partially successful effort to predict, while the economy was on the downgrade of a business cycle, how severe that recession was likely to be. This experiment dealt with the cycle which passed the peak and started down in July 1957.

As a standard of comparison, Moore chose the contraction phase of seven previous business cycles, arranged in order of severity from mild to severe, as in Table 5.

TABLE 5

Contraction	*Rank*
Oct. 1926-Nov. 1927	1 (mildest)
July 1953-Aug. 1954	2
Nov. 1948-Oct. 1949	3
May 1923-July 1924	4
Jan. 1920-July 1921	5
May 1937-June 1938	6
Aug. 1929-Mar. 1933	7 (most severe)

The first step in the analysis was to discover, for each of these contractions, "how much business activity declined from the peak as the contraction continued, and compare such measures with the above ranking." This showed "how many months after the contractions began the relative severity of each recession became evident, and how it manifested itself in different aspects of economic activity, such as production, employment, incomes, prices. Similar measures constructed during the course of a current contraction can then be used to appraise its severity and its scope compared with earlier contractions."

The analysis indicated the following tentative conclusions, among others:

After the first six months of a recession the percentage fall in most economic aggregates (such as employment, production, etc.) is smaller in mild recessions than in the more severe, and this ranking is maintained with little change thereafter.

When the same comparisons are made in the leading series (which turn down before the peak) the difference between severe and mild contractions appears about four months after the recession begins, and continues thereafter.

Both mild and sharp contractions have sometimes ended within a year, but the previous peak level is regained more quickly after a mild contraction.

Forecasts made on such evidence may turn out to be mistaken because of unforeseen factors—such as governmental measures to combat the depression.

Using material of this kind, Moore concluded in February 1958 (six months after a recession began), and published in a report which went to press in April 1958, that the recession would probably turn out to be milder than the worst three in the above list, and less mild than the mildest three. Subsequent developments confirmed this forecast.

The report, however, did not precisely pinpoint the magnitude of the recession and was only partially successful in forecasting its duration. The whole cycle, from peak to peak, was expected to occupy between eighteen and twenty-four months. According to one measure (the Federal Reserve index of industrial production), it did last twenty months, but according to another method, based on a number of coincidental indicators, the duration of the cycle was only sixteen months. For a pioneering experiment of this sort, however, it was at worst a near miss.

Applications of the Discoveries

The National Bureau of Economic Research, which carried on the careful studies briefly summarized here, does not publish regular forecasts. Since it is a scientific, noncommercial organization, its function is to collect, test, and analyze data, to arrive at and revise conclusions that best interpret the facts, and to publish reports of its research, not only in the business cycle, but in other fields of public importance. Once the underlying data are analyzed and tested, and the results made known, the bureau leaves to others the task of applying them.

This had been the case with its pioneering research which developed the concepts and accounts of the national income. After the basic work was done, the bureau passed on to the United States Department of Commerce the task of calculating and publishing current figures in that large realm.

A similar policy has been applied to business-cycle forecasting. The arduous task of keeping up to date the figures of the various indicators and diffusion indexes, and of publishing them currently, has been taken over by the Department of Commerce, while the National Bureau concentrates its efforts on the research frontier, which may add to existing knowledge. Any citizen who wants the current facts can obtain them in a monthly publication of the United States Government, *Business Cycle Developments.*

The Department of Commerce, however, does not itself publish forecasts based on the data that it distributes. For the present at least, it is content to supply to any and all comers the relevant material, so that any institution or individual may use it in attempting to foresee the economic weather. In this way it escapes the possible responsibility for a forecast which could be regarded as having political overtones, or for making a mistake which could cause losses or disappointments for which government might be blamed. No doubt it might do as well in forecasting as the Weather Bureau, but after all, people are used to accepting risks and unpleasant surprises which come from the atmosphere, whereas they are likely to blame governmental authorities for the vagaries of human behavior.

The National Bureau, however, is at this writing engaged in a project which may help the individual citizen to recognize relatively good forecasting and to know what limitations to expect. It is analyzing forecasts actually made by institutions which have published their conclusions, in order to discover which methods are the more reliable, which are the less, and the reasons in both cases. This should add to the scientifically validated information which it has already offered to the public.

In addition, of course, the bureau continues its own studies in the field, in order to deepen and broaden what is already known, and to keep pace with any changes that may occur. The task of science is never-ending in any realm; this is particularly true of the sciences dealing with human societies, which change from decade to decade, and sometimes even from year to year. But the task in this instance at least is not thankless, because what has already been discovered can be used to influence intelligent choice and use of methods to dampen, though probably not to abolish, the blight of cyclical depressions.

SIX

HOW MONEY APPEARS AND DISAPPEARS

For many years the succession of good times and bad times was supposed by large sections of the public, and by many students of economics as well, to be due almost entirely to changes in the supply of money. The history of the United States is checkered with political controversies between those who wanted to restrict the amount in order to safeguard property-holders against inflation, and others who needed more money and argued that either government or the banks ought to supply it. Was it not obvious that unemployment, or low prices for farm produce, or failure of land held by speculators to advance in value, was due to insufficient money in the hands of potential buyers?

Such controversies occurred during the history of the First and the Second Bank of the United States, and in the post-Civil War arguments over the Greenbacks and the proposal for free and unlimited coinage of silver. Even during the 1920s a formidable movement arose, supported by eminent economists, who held that the monetary supply ought to be kept at a quantity just adequate to keep prices steady, on the theory that depression was caused by falling prices, and price inflation followed too much money. Prices of commodities and services were unusually steady between 1923 and 1929, and this phenomenon led some economists mistakenly to assume that the economy as a whole must be in a healthy state.

Money is indeed important, and the policies of those who control it should be carefully adjusted to the needs of the economy, but persons who regarded its quantity as the principal determinant of economic health overlooked an important fact. Not merely the quantity of money, but the speed of its circulation—the flow of actual spending and its balance with the volume of goods and services offered for sale—is the critical consideration. The attention of economists has been, in recent years, focused more on income, spending, and investment than on the tokens of one kind or another that are used as the medium of exchange.

Money flows around and around, from consumers to business and government, from business and government back to consumers. (Money here is used in the broad sense to include not merely coins and "folding money" but also bank deposits, which are paid out by checks.) For any given period, total expenditure must equal total income. If as much is always received as is spent (including investment), and as much is always spent as is received, how is it possible for income and spending ever to change? How does the income, which constitutes demand, ever get bigger or smaller? Experience tells us that it does.

The puzzle is something like that propounded centuries ago by the Greek philosopher Zeno about motion. A modern illustration of Zeno's puzzle might be as follows. Suppose you are equipped with a camera with a very fast lens and shutter. You take a picture of a runner doing the hundred-yard dash. This picture shows him at a given position on the track. No matter at what instant you take the picture, he will appear to be at one point or another. Even a movie film is a succession of pictures of the runner at a series of fixed points. How does he ever get from one point to the next? Where does the motion come in?

The answer is of course that for the sake of our "instantaneous pictures" we deliberately eliminate as much of the motion as we can in order to obtain a clear outline of our subject. If we left the shutter open, we should get a picture of the motion all right, but the runner would appear as a blur. The same is true of economic tables showing income and spending. Both income and spending actually change from day to day; we simply take a snapshot covering a single period at a time so that the picture may be clear.

In the case of money, however, we still have to account for the source of expansion or contraction when its volume changes.

Government as a Source of Money

Government can easily increase the amount of coins or

paper money, and can do so without regard to the number of things produced. This can happen even if there is a rigid gold standard. On various occasions in the world's history new discoveries of gold, which could be sold by the miners to the government at a fixed money value per ounce, have increased the amount of money available and thus have led to booms. If a government departs from the gold or other metallic standard, it can pay its bills merely by running the printing press; this has happened many times.

Government can also reduce the amount of money in circulation by various devices, though this process is more difficult and less often resorted to. By heavy taxes it can build up a surplus and then destroy paper money collected or withhold money of any kind from further circulation. Or it can call in existing paper money, announcing that the old currency will cease to be legal tender as of a certain date. The money turned in is exchanged for new currency of lower denomination. For instance, the holder of a two-dollar bill might get for it a dollar of the new money. This is a method of enforcing devaluation, which has been practiced mainly after wars.

So-called budgetary inflation can occur when the government does not collect enough revenue from the public to pay its bills and covers the deficit by expanding the money supply. It is a mistake, however, to assume that this practice will always lead to rapidly rising prices. When there is a large volume of unemployment and much idle industrial capacity, increase of money in circulation is likely to result in more production and employment. Only when full capacity for production is approached will prices rise very much, because only then will the means of payment grow more rapidly than production. During wars the labor supply is reduced by military service, and the demand for munitions is so large that production soon reaches the limit of capacity. Then, unless government collects from the public all it spends, as governments almost never do during wars, the money spent will be enlarged more rapidly than the goods and services produced.

Banks as a Source of Money

Government is not the only source of money in modern economics. Anybody who can borrow from a bank sometimes obtains purchasing power which neither he nor anybody else had before. If bank loans as a whole are extended faster than they are paid off, the supply of money (or deposits, which amount to the same thing) increases. When bank loans as a whole are paid off faster than they are extended, the supply of money inevitably decreases.

This may sound fallacious to anyone who has an elementary conception of the way banks operate. The ordinary supposition is that somebody with extra money deposits it in a bank; the bank then can lend this money to somebody else. How can loans be made if the money is not previously in existence? They can and are; anybody who wants to verify the fact can look at the tables in the *Federal Reserve Bulletin* and see how the total of bank loans changes from time to time.

When deposits grow, the reason is largely that borrowings have grown; the chain of causation ordinarily runs from loans to deposits rather than the other way. Somebody borrows from a bank; the bank adds to his deposit account the proceeds of the loan. If he draws it out by issuing checks, the amount by which his deposit is reduced appears as an addition to the bank accounts of those who receive the checks. The money loaned remains in circulation—either in deposits or in currency. When total borrowings from the banks are reduced, deposits (or currency) shrink by an equal amount. Nowadays, in the United States, many more payments are made by check than by currency.

Banks do not expect all depositors to withdraw their money at the same time. That is why the banking system as a whole can lend more money than it holds in cash. Suppose, to make the process clear, that there were in the country only one big bank. It could lend with impunity, say, six times as much as its reserve of cash. While some people draw out money, others deposit it. The reserve acts as a margin of safety. The bulk of withdrawals and deposits consists not of currency but of mere entries on the books. The borrower draws a check on the bank and sends it to his creditor, who promptly deposits the check. Bank loans have thus been increased, but the lending bank has the same amount of money in its reserve as it had when the process started.

The same process operates in our system of many banks, because a withdrawal by check from one bank will almost certainly be followed by deposit of the check either in that or in some other bank, which can collect from the bank on which the check was drawn. As withdrawals and deposits work their way around the system, each bank's reserves are replenished.

Of course there must be some safe limit to the ratio between reserves and bank loans. A minimum limit is enforced by law, but even if it were not, good banking practice would recognize it because of past experience. If the public loses confidence in the ability of a bank to meet its obligation it will draw out deposits in cash and hoard the money. Then the bank will be in real trouble. This lack of confidence became general in 1932-1933; the result was that all banks had to be closed until confidence could be restored.

When production of goods is growing and more people are being employed, business is likely to need to borrow more from the banks. But there is very little assurance that when bank loans expand, and in consequence the total of demand grows, the production of goods and services will go on indefinitely increasing by the same amount. When the country is producing all it can, with its existing supply of materials, machinery, and labor, loans may still increase. The mere fact that businesses need more money with which to buy goods and pay wages does not always mean that production and employment are increasing correspondingly. Sometimes the need for additional bank credit merely reflects rising prices.

In an inflationary period the interaction of prices and bank credit is much like the behavior of an airplane motor which runs by a jet of hot gas expelled from its stern. The gas is produced by a combination of compressed air and burning kerosene or similar fuel. The motor takes in air through its snout; its speed compresses the air; the more highly compressed the air, the more powerful is the jet. Thus (within limits, of course) it is said of the plane that the faster it goes, the faster it goes. Similarly, unchecked expansion of bank credit may boost prices; higher prices in turn increase the need for bank credit.

Nor is there any assurance that when the total of bank loans decreases they will fall only to the point where there is still enough demand to keep everybody employed at capacity production. You may have a factory capable of making a hundred washing machines a day and employing five thousand persons to do it. But your sales may fall to eighty a day and your employment to four thousand. If you had larger loans from the bank, you could make more, but if you are a prudent manager you will not borrow in order to make more than you think you can sell, and if you are not a prudent manager the bank probably will not lend you the money anyway.

Central Banks and the Money Supply

In all modern nations there are institutions which act as banks for the banks which lend money to the public. This fact makes possible some unified control over the expansion or contraction of the supply of money.

In the United States the central banks are called Federal Reserve Banks; there are twelve of them, each covering a certain district. All are under the jurisdiction of a single board of governors. In most other countries there is only a single central bank, such as the Bank of England or the Bank of France.

An American bank which belongs to the Federal Reserve System (all national banks must belong to it, and many state banks belong as well) must deposit its reserve with the Federal Reserve Bank of its district, keeping such cash as it needs for day-to-day operations. It can then borrow from the Federal Reserve Bank in order to lend more to its own customers. The maximum amount it can borrow is of course limited by the size of its reserve.

The Federal Reserve Board is granted by the government the power to issue paper money. Look at the bills in your pocketbook and you will find that, with the exception of some for one or two dollars, most of them are labeled "Federal Reserve Note." When a bank borrows paper money from a Federal Reserve Bank, this is the kind of money it gets.

A bank cannot borrow from a Reserve Bank just by asking for the loan or an advance. It usually has to put up collateral. Of course, when it gets any gold, it can obtain money or credit for that. A note signed by a businessman or a farmer who has borrowed is good collateral. Thus, if the Federal Reserve consents to lend it enough, a bank can keep on lending without depleting its money supply at all. It simply endorses notes in its possession, sends them into the Reserve Bank, and receives from the Reserve Bank enough to lend just as much again. It must pay interest for these loans—at a rate somewhat below the rate it charges the customer. The interest rate charged by the Reserve Bank is called the "discount rate." By raising the discount rate, the Reserve Bank can do something to discourage borrowing; by lowering it, something to encourage the expansion of credit. Change in the discount rate is one of the powers of Reserve

Banks to influence the volume of money. But the Reserve Banks cannot by this means force the commercial banks to borrow or to lend.

Far more effective than changing the discount rate is the Reserve Bank's purchase or sale of securities. Suppose a Reserve Bank buys a thousand-dollar government bond. (It is not allowed to buy private bonds.) If it buys the bond from a bank, the payment immediately gives the bank $1,000 more, in its deposit with the Reserve Bank. The selling bank can lend more money accordingly. If the Reserve Bank buys the bond from some person or company, the seller probably deposits the proceeds in a bank, and the same expansion of reserves occurs. The initiative in buying or selling bonds lies with the Reserve Banks; the initiative in discounting lies with the member banks.

When the Reserve Bank sells bonds, the checks (or currency) paid by the buyers reduce bank reserves, and the power of banks to lend is correspondingly reduced. Changes in the size of bank reserves may change the amount of loans which the banks can make by as much as six times.

Still another power of the Reserve Bank authorities, seldom used because it is so drastic, is to change up or down the legal minimum ratio between the reserves of the commercial banks and the outstanding loans.

This power of Reserve Banks to make money appear or disappear is not unlimited. Their loans and the currency in circulation in combination cannot, according to law, exceed four times their gold reserve. (The gold itself must be turned over to the United States Treasury, which exchanges for it gold certificates to be held by the Reserve Bank.) They can increase the reserves of the member banks by buying bonds, but if the member banks do not lend a larger amount to the public, the money supply is not increased. Banks often do not lend all they legally can, especially in depressions. Those business concerns which need the money or think they can make profitable use of it may not enjoy good credit standing at such times. In time of prosperity and active demand for loans, the Reserve Banks can usually restrict lending by selling bonds. But even then, if a lot of gold is coming into the country to pay for exports, the banks which receive it have correspondingly increased reserves, and thus may counteract the effect of restriction caused by any Reserve Bank selling. (They must hand the gold over to the Reserve Banks, but of course they are credited with it.)

Government Power to Increase Bank Credit

Government *can* increase the supply of money by printing it, but most modern governments don't act so crudely any more. The government, during a war or a depression, has to spend more money than it is collecting. It borrows the money, giving the lender a note or bond. On the surface, this looks like an ordinary business transaction; it does not arouse the alarm which would result if the government simply printed a lot of money to pay its bills. If the lender is an individual or a company, and if he puts the bond away in his strong box and takes the money out of his bank account to pay for it, it *is* an ordinary business transaction and does not enlarge the amount of purchasing power. The buyer's deposit is decreased; the government's deposit is increased by the same amount; total deposits remain the same.

But suppose the purchaser of the bond goes to the bank and borrows enough to buy it. Then his bank deposit remains intact; the government's deposit is increased by the amount he pays for the bond, and the volume of money jumps a dollar for every dollar the government borrows. If a bank "buys" the bond, the bank lends directly to the government instead of to some bond buyer. Bank deposits are increased in either case, and the immediate effect is exactly the same as if the government had printed the money it spent instead of borrowing it.

Central banks almost invariably buy government bonds in periods of emergency. (Central banks are either directly or indirectly under government control.) By buying bonds the central banks give the other banks all the reserves they need to extend credit. Central-bank buying also helps to keep up the price of the bonds so that the government will not have to offer a high rate of interest.

Thus government and the banking system in combination constitute a powerful means of increasing the supply of money. Government, in wars and depressions, as well as sometimes in other circumstances, spends more than it receives; the bank loans to which its borrowing immediately gives rise enlarge the general purchasing power; the purchases of government bonds by central banks enlarge bank reserves and permit the banks to increase the means of payment still more by means of lending to private borrowers.

Between December 1941 and December 1947, the period of World War II and the first two years after its end, marketable United States government obligations grew by about 120 billion dollars. Of these, commercial banks held at the latter date about 60 billion and Federal Reserve Banks 20 billion. This accounts for the increase in purchasing power which occurred. Deposits and currency in circulation together grew by about 90 billion in the same period. The total of deposits and circulating money at the beginning of 1948 was more than twice as great as seven years earlier. This was the primary source of inflation.

During the depression of the 1930s the government pursued the same financial policy as it did in the subsequent war, though its borrowing and spending were on a far smaller scale. There was some increase of money as a result, but not enough to eliminate unemployment. And because production did not grow to the level of capacity or even near it, prices did not rise markedly. For one reason or another, private borrowers did not make use of all the credit which the increased bank reserves would have made possible. Opinions differ as to what the reason was.

During the war bank loans did not grow so much as the increase in bank reserves would have permitted. This was largely the result of governmental controls of wages and prices. When these controls were removed in 1946, prices began to shoot up. Even at the beginning of 1948 further expansion of money and deposits was possible, on the basis of the existing bank reserves. And the Reserve Banks could increase these reserves still further by continuing to purchase government bonds.

Government Power to Decrease Bank Credit

When the government has added to the money supply by printing, it can reduce the supply again by collecting in taxes more than it spends. The same principle applies when the government has increased money by the modern process of borrowing. In this case, when it has a surplus of receipts over expenditures, it may reduce the supply of money by paying off some of its loans.

But the second process is more complicated. When the government redeems a bond from an individual owner the government's funds are reduced, but the seller's are increased by the same amount. The volume of bank deposits plus money in circulation therefore remains the same. In order to force a reduction of purchasing power in this way, the government has to do something to reduce the banks' desire or power to lend.

Again it comes back to what the central bank does. The central bank must *sell* government securities as the government buys them if the money paid by the government is automatically to disappear. In that case, the proceeds of the sales (deposits or money) find their resting place in the central bank, which does not put them into circulation again. As long as the central bank is selling, it is reducing the reserves of the banks which lend to private borrowers, so that they are likely to lend less.

Since governments nowadays control central-bank policy, this result is comparatively easy to bring about. But the government must as a rule pay a price for it. When the government was selling the bonds, it maintained the price by central-bank buying. Thus it obtained a low rate of interest. But later, if the central bank were to sell instead of buying, the price of bonds might fall and the rate of interest would rise correspondingly. This means that in the future the government would have to pay more interest on a given amount of debt. This might be a serious burden on the budget and hence on the taxpayers. Banks and many private business concerns are also faced with a problem because of the fact that a large part of their assets consists of bonds, which will fall in value if large quantities are offered for sale.

For this and other reasons governments seldom deflate the money supply as much as they have inflated it. Serious deflation sometimes happens without anyone's planning it, but when governments exercise deliberate policy in the matter they usually are content to stop inflation, if they can, by making sure that no *more* money is added, instead of withdrawing large amounts from circulation and bringing about drastic cuts in prices. Serious deflation of this kind is adopted, as a rule, only when inflation has proceeded to extremes and an entirely new currency has to be substituted for the old.

Banks Are the Storage Reservoirs

Thus, in a modern economy, the banking system is the ultimate origin of extra money added to the flow of purchasing power, and the ultimate recipient of money withdrawn from it. Banks are somewhat like the storage reservoirs in a river system. When more water is needed, the gates may be opened; when less is wanted, the gates may be shut. Thus something can be done to counteract floods or droughts.

Government can take the initiative in opening or shutting the banking gates, and usually does so in wars or other great emergencies. It can increase the flow by borrowing and spending; it can decrease the flow by paying off its loans.

But in a system in which government is not the only source of spending—that is, in a system in which private enterprise plays an important role—government action does not usually suffice to regulate the flow in time of peace. What consumers and business concerns borrow and spend determines a large part of the flow of money and income. The banking system can do something to regulate this flow, but, on the whole, the banks are more passive than active in control of the flow of credit and money. In time of depression they cannot lend money which solvent borrowers do not want to borrow or cannot offer good security for. In time of great business activity and rising prices they have difficulty in preventing an increase of deposits and loans, unless government and central banks take a firm initiative.

There still remains the question why at some times the private sector of the economy borrows less than enough to keep the machines busy and employment high, and why at other times it borrows more than enough and so produces speculative rises in prices.

SEVEN

ECONOMIC EDUCATION OF THE PEOPLE

No matter how much specialists in economic science may know about the behavior of economic forces, cycles, or forecasting, and no matter how potent are the instruments which may be used to stabilize the economy, such as central-banking policy and governmental fiscal policy, these instruments are not likely to be used efficiently in a democratic nation unless the people understand at least some of the principles involved and elect to public office candidates who are capable of understanding at least as much as the citizens who elect them. The American people did learn a great deal about economic policies from their experience in the fabulous 1920s, the tragic 1930s, and the period of the Second World War. They learned it largely in the hard way. This chapter is chiefly concerned with the economic education of the nation between 1920 and 1945.

The "New Era" of the 1920s

Before 1917, a movement for reform in the United States endeavored to remove corruption in government and remedy injustices in the social order. "Big business" became suspect. President Theodore Roosevelt had tried to reform the national Republican party and failing in that, had split the organization with his effort to launch a new and regenerative Progressive party. The Democrats in 1912 had nominated and elected to the Presidency a former university professor of political science, who had later become in turn President of

Princeton and Governor of New Jersey. In less than two years President Woodrow Wilson had, with the help of the more enlightened members of Congress, achieved the passage of a distinguished body of new legislation, including the establishment of the Federal Reserve System, a progressive income tax, new anti-trust measures, and reduction of the high protective tariff.

War broke out in Europe in August 1914 and thereafter involved the United States deeply in economic support of the belligerents. After an effort to remain neutral, this country entered the conflict in April 1917. The American nation almost overnight had to become a directed and planned economy—though in some cases it was poorly planned. It won the war, but many Americans believed it lost the peace by the Treaty of Versailles. The old spirit of isolationism came to vigorous life. The United States declined to join the League of Nations. Soldiers and sailors, war workers in the mills and factories, their families, businessmen and bankers, were sick of the whole adventure. So it happened that when in 1920 the "Old Guard" in the Republican Party nominated for President a right-wing senator, Warren G. Harding, and he adopted as his slogan "Return to normalcy," he was elected by a wide majority.

Almost everybody understood that most businessmen, and especially big businessmen, were orthodox Republicans and that the party would now serve mainly business interests by orthodox methods. Progressive views and reforms were in the discard. The new administration promptly increased protective import duties, appointed as Secretary of the Treasury one of the richest men in the nation—Andrew Mellon—and drastically reduced taxes on profits and incomes, making the larger cuts on the higher brackets. It emasculated administration of the anti-trust laws. Though its record became tarnished by bribery and corruption under Mr. Harding—discovered after his death—his successor, Vice-President Calvin Coolidge, won a reputation for honesty, for penurious federal spending, and for the taciturnity of the sort to be expected from a Vermonter. In year after year, the federal budget was balanced. Nevertheless, the national administration did make large expenditures to help business—such as subsidies for an economically inefficient shipping industry and a youthful aviation industry. Federal funds stimulated highway construction for the first time since the early years of the nineteenth century—an activity necessary for the growth of a still youthful automobile industry. At the same time, the President stubbornly refused to sanction any of the proposals urged by farmers to raise the prices of crops—which had fallen far more than the prices of the goods farmers had to buy—or to remove obstacles in the path of labor organization and collective bargaining. Everyone understood that "normalcy" meant supremacy for private business enterprise in the United States, coupled with political isolation from the rest of the world.

After a sharp fall of prices in 1921—the year in which Harding was inaugurated—the economy took off for a period of rapid growth, scarcely interrupted by mild recessions in 1924 and in 1926-1927. New or relatively new industries expanded year after year to supply their steadily widening markets—radio, automobile, synthetic fabrics, household electric appliances such as vacuum cleaners, refrigerators, and kitchen ranges. Better engineering and scientific management boosted factory output 32 per cent per man-hour between 1923 and 1929. The scarcity of housing consequent to the previous war was more than remedied. Prices of consumer goods remained steady; consumers spent more and more—their purchases were 23 per cent larger in 1929 than in 1923. Prices of shares on the stock exchanges rose year after year; almost anybody could make quick gains by buying shares (often with the aid of margin loans) and selling them not much later at a higher price.

Private enterprise was "working"; it produced some benefits for almost everybody—though the gains were much greater in the upper-income brackets than in the lower ones. Large majorities consistently returned to federal office the candidates of the party which had introduced the "New Era." Spokesmen for the regime became jubilant.

In December 1928 President Coolidge wrote in his final message to Congress: "No Congress of the United States ever assembled, in surveying the state of the Union, has met with a more pleasing prospect than that which appears at the present time. . . . The great wealth created by our enterprise and industry, and saved by our economy, has had the widest distribution among our own people, and has gone out in a steady stream to serve the charity and the business of the world. . . . The country can regard the present with satisfaction and the future with optimism." President Herbert Hoover had been elected in the autumn of 1928 with the slogan, "A chicken in every pot and two cars in every garage."

During Mr. Hoover's first year in office the stock market

suffered probably the worst panic in the history of the nation, and the Great Depression of the 1930s began.

Disillusion in the 1930s

The old story of the speculative excesses and fantastic frauds that occurred in the financial markets of the 1920s need not here be repeated. Perhaps the most revealing development of the latter years of the decade was that large business enterprises discovered that they could make more profits by lending their ready cash, in the form of margin loans, to speculators in the shares of their companies, than by using the money to expand production in the goods and services which they sold. Thus a large share of the credit which was blown into the speculative bubble came not from the banks, which were under some public control through the Federal Reserve System, but from these "others," as they were designated in the statistical figures. And the rapid calling of loans by business lenders as soon as prices began to fall was an important factor in the collapse of the stock market.

A prevailing delusion was that after the panic in Wall Street was over all would be well; business in general was "fundamentally sound." Stock prices would "bottom out." More credit would be available for legitimate business. All that was necessary was to restore business confidence. Restoration of confidence required that the budget of the federal government be balanced, and, as usual, that government should not interfere with private enterprise. As in previous recessions, the weaker enterprises would be eliminated, and a new equilibrium would result from the automatic adjustment of prices and costs in a competitive economy.

President Hoover understood and accepted this orthodox theory. Men out of work would regain their jobs when wages had been reduced to the point where it would be profitable to employ them, and when business confidence was restored. In the meantime the federal budget must not be burdened with "doles" to the jobless; their needs must be served by local governments or private philanthropy. The President and other federal officials made frequent encouraging forecasts: prosperity was "just around the corner." Then the "New Era" could continue to enrich the American people and the world.

What really was around the corner looked, when it arrived, more like collapse of the capitalist system. Between the autumn of 1929 and March 1933, when Mr. Hoover's term of office had expired, the ranks of the unemployed became nearly one-fourth of the labor force (which includes everyone who receives, or is looking for, any recompense for work in the form of wages, salaries, or profits earned by farmers and other individual proprietors such as small businessmen and members of the professions). Rates of wages of those who still had jobs had been repeatedly cut, while most of them were working only part time. The drastic reduction of earnings paid to the working forces sharply reduced the demand for the goods and services produced. All governmental budgets, including that of the federal government, were hopelessly in the red because of falling tax receipts. Local governments, plus private philanthropy, could scarcely provide enough food for the unemployed, not to speak of shelter. Some cities could not pay firemen, policemen, or teachers. Thousands of farmers were losing their land by mortgage foreclosure or tax sales. In some instances, groups of farmers with loaded shotguns prevented such auctions. And, in the last months of the Hoover administration, depositors, losing confidence in the solvency of the banks, withdrew so much cash that in numerous states all the banks had to be closed.

The voters elected, in November 1932, the Democratic candidate, Franklin D. Roosevelt, not because they understood the measures he advocated, but because apparently he would do something new and represented opposition to the Hoover policy. In March 1933, when Mr. Roosevelt took office, he promised vigorous action. Immediately he became as good as his word by closing all the banks and announcing that only those that were sound would be permitted to reopen. Congress promptly passed the requisite legislation. This reassurance ended the runs on banks; cash formerly withdrawn was redeposited, and even gold flowed back to them. Within a few weeks about three-fourths of the banks had been saved. Mr. Roosevelt—who certainly was no expert in economics but was willing to take advice from experts, and above all was a superb politician in the better sense of the word—had within a month prompted more confidence in the minds of the citizens than Mr. Hoover's policy had induced in four years. The beginning of recovery, according to the economic statisticians who specialize in the business cycle, occurred in the spring of 1933.

This object lesson in what could be done by the federal government if it did positively intervene in economic affairs made a deep impression on the citizens. During his first two terms in office Mr. Roosevelt advocated and won popular support for a long list of measures which enlisted governmental participation in the attempt to reshape and strengthen the economy. Not all these measures were well conceived; some were subsequently abandoned. It is not relevant to the argument of this chapter to assess their several merits or demerits. The pertinent conclusion concerns rather the change in the attitude of the American people. They were convinced that they had been, in the end, poorly served by "normalcy" and by the "New Era," which, they had been assured, had been dominated by untrammeled business. Now, in spite of the fact that spokesmen of organized business bitterly opposed many of the new measures and sometimes even declined to obey them, a large majority of the voters had become convinced by their experience that governmental intervention does, and must, play an important role in the economy. This mood has become firmly implanted in the tradition and often as well in the contemporary action of the nation.

The Dilemma of the Economists

Those professional economists who in the 1920s and early 1930s had been immersed in the classical theory were unprepared to deal with the collapse of the national economy which took place before their eyes. As citizens and human beings many of them felt as strongly as the untutored masses that drastic measures must be taken to relieve the unemployed and reverse the downward spiral. Numerous measures to boost employment had been proposed by writers not under the spell of the classical theory—measures such as a large program of public works. But almost all the proposed remedies involved governmental intervention, and the adherents of the dominant theory felt uneasy in abandoning the framework of ideas which, in the abstract, had been logically and carefully developed. They needed a new body of theory to justify what they wanted to recommend.

According to the classical theory, there is not "naturally" any possibility of a shortage of demand. The money which is paid out in the process of production and sale must equal the amount necessary to buy the product. When troubles arise, they are caused merely by temporary obstructions to the normal operations of competition and to the balancing of supply and demand of particular kinds of goods through the mechanism of prices. The adherent of this theory simply says,

"Get rid of monopoly and other aritificial regulations or interferences, and all will be well." More simply said than done!

An appropriate new theory was just being developed by a well-known British economist, John Maynard Keynes, who had been educated in the classical tradition and, among numerous distinguished activities, had taught economics at Cambridge University. Though his complete statement of the new doctrine—*The General Theory of Employment, Interest and Money*—was not published until 1936, he had previously made known his views in other publications accessible to the economic fraternity. He proved to the satisfaction of many of his readers that a level of full employment is not the "natural" state of things at all.

The accepted theory, he argued, was adapted to a special case—the case in which it was assumed that prices would respond easily to changes in supply and demand, and that something like perfect competition in fact existed. But that was not the real world. There were trade unions; there were powerful business organizations. Resistance by labor to reduction of wages and by business to reduction of prices customarily occurred. He proposed a theory which would embrace the real world—a general theory.

We have seen that total national income always equals total spending plus investment, but that nevertheless income does change from time to time. Keynes argued that these changes take place largely through differences between the amount invested and the amount people refrain from spending with the intention of saving it.

Let us take an oversimplified example to illustrate the point. Suppose national income is $100. Suppose that of this amount consumers spend $90 for consumer goods, while the other $10 is laid aside by individuals and business in combination. Now, suppose business invests in inventory, machinery, plant, and houses, not only the $10 saved but $5 in addition. (It might do so by borrowing from the banks.) Thus, spending plus investment becomes $105. This, in turn, equals the national income. The national income has grown from $100 to $105.

Or suppose, on the contrary, that while $10 of a $100 national income was being withheld from the purchase of consumer goods, business invested only $5. Only $95 would thus be spent and invested, and the national income would have shrunk to $95.

The crucial point of the Keynes theory, which differentiates it from the classical view, is that equilibrium between total demand and total supply may be reached at a point of demand which is too low to maintain full employment and capacity production. The classical theory argued that the economy was always approximating equilibrium at a full-employment level. The only things which could prevent it from remaining at this level were "frictions" and "rigidities" in the competitive price mechanism. Keynes held that, frictions or no frictions, equilibrium might be reached at a level which permitted unemployment.

The practical consequences of this conclusion are diametrically opposed to those which flow from the classical one. If you assume that the natural state of equilibrium is one of full employment, and departures from it are due to interferences with competitive private enterprise, then you must conclude that intervention by government is just as harmful as any other kind of intervention. In that case, government ought to refrain from spending to maintain employment, from fixing minimum wages, or from other forms of regulation. If, on the other hand, you believe, as Keynes did, that equilibrium may be reached at a level of activity where unemployment is prevalent, you would argue, as Keynes did, that government ought to make up for any deficiency of private investment by spending funds which it did not take from consumers.

In Keynesian terms, spending by the government *is* investment. When government spends money for buildings, roads, education, or other improvements, it adds something to the wealth of the nation, just as would investments by private business. Therefore, when government spends more than it collects—in other words, has a deficit—it is exerting exactly the same influence in expanding the national income as do private business concerns when they invest more than is saved. In both cases the source of the extra investment is borrowing. And, when government has a surplus in its budget, it is saving, just as do private citizens and business firms when they spend less than they earn.

From this analysis it is easy to justify the use of governmental fiscal policy to stabilize the ups and downs of a private-enterprise economy. A deficit in governmental finance will increase the money in the hands of the citizens, since government will be spending more than it is collecting. This is desirable in a recession. A surplus in governmental budgets, on the other hand, will take more money from the citizens than is paid out to them. This is desirable when people are trying to buy more than the economy can produce, thus forcing up prices. The policy may be used as a curb on inflation.

Why is it that, in the private sector of the economy, an equilibrium may be reached at a point where there is an abnormal amount of unemployment? According to the Keynes theory, it can happen that business spends for new buildings, equipment, and stocks of goods less money than people as a whole divert from their purchase of consumer goods with the intention of saving it. If this happens, there will be a slump of employment, because there will be shrinkage in spending plus investment. Incomes will fall, people will be compelled to spend for living expenses what they have "saved," or to save less, or both. In this case, the amount of money being withheld from current spending will soon shrink to the amount being invested. The opposite process takes place if business spends more for capital than people are withholding from expenditure. Employment will rise, incomes will increase, and more money will be withheld from consumption until the amount "saved" again equals what is being invested.

Saving in the national accounts must be identical with investment. Saving in the colloquial sense of what people refrain from spending with the intention of saving it may for a time be larger or smaller than investment, but, according to Keynes, it will follow the trend of investment and in the end will equal it. At that point "equilibrium" occurs.

Criticisms of the Keynes Theory

It is important to understand that while Keynes upset the classical notion of a natural equilibrium at full employment, he was trained in the classical way of thinking and phrased his theory in terms of an equilibrium of his own. In developing this theory, he dealt almost as little with the real world of monopolistic and other restrictions of the markets as did the older theorists whom he was attacking. Both he and they were talking not so much about what really does happen, as revealed by measurement of economic statistics, but about what logically must happen, given certain assumptions or premises, which may not correspond with the actual world.

In this sense the Keynes theory is a hypothesis which needs testing, rather than a final truth. It may be that the economic order does not naturally seek equilibrium at any point, high or low. It may be that the fluctuations of investment do not play the decisive role Keynes assigned to them. It is true that, according to the statistics, investment does fluctuate more widely than purchases of consumer goods in general. But it is also true that the outlay for consumer goods makes up a much larger part of the total flow of income than does investment, so that a small percentage variation in this part can be a much larger factor in changes of total income than the larger percentage variation in investment.

Nor is it necessary to assume that changes in consumer spending spring largely from changes in consumer income, as Keynes appears to do. When people spend so large a part of their incomes as in recent years for durable goods such as automobiles, their demand for new cars may be financed by an expansion of consumer borrowing, or it may approach its limit and begin to fall off without any prior decline in their aggregate income. It is quite possible that consumer durable goods may play a role in fluctuations of demand that Keynes assigned to business investment. They are, in a sense, an important form of "savings" and "investment" themselves.

Before leaving the Keynes theory, we should perhaps learn to recognize one or two of the technical terms which he introduced, since they frequently recur in the discussions of economists.

"Propensity to consume" means the habit of spending a certain part of one's income for consumer goods. Keynes assumed that this was a fairly stable habit; savings made out of income at any one income level, he thought, would remain a certain percentage of that level. The larger the income, the higher the percentage of saving. A given amount of additional investment would immediately increase the income of the recipients by that amount. As the recipients spent money, the income of those who received it on the second round would be accordingly increased, but not by so much as on the first round, because those on the first round would have saved (not spent) some of their additional income. And so it would continue as the income "injected" by a given amount of investment made its way around the economy. On the basis of this logic, if one knew both the "marginal propensity to consume"—that is, the percentage of the additional income that would be spent by those who received it—and the amount of increase in investment which started the process, one could calculate the "multiplier" by which the amount of the new investment must be multiplied in order to discover the much larger amount by which the national income would be increased.

But the "propensity to consume" may not be so stable at each level of income as Keynes supposed. And the "multiplier" did not work as it theoretically should have done after 1933. Deficit spending by government during the New Deal had much less effect in increasing national income than one would have expected on the basis of the multiplier formula. Adherents of the Keynes theory explained this discrepancy by the fact that most businessmen were opposed to the New Deal and did not understand the possible boost to the economy which deficit spending might trigger. Cooperation by the business community was, of course, essential in any such economic revival as the Keynes theory seemed to make possible. Only through decisions to invest more in private business could full recovery be attained.

The Effect on Popular Opinion

The Keynes theory took effect mainly in easing the minds of economists about federal relief of unemployment at the expense of governmental deficits. Probably the President never understood it and in any case was not greatly motivated by theoretical considerations. Certainly most of the people who benefited from the measures adopted to relieve unemployment were not adept in economic analysis. But their common sense, applied to their experience, taught them that only the federal government did, and apparently could under the circumstances, come to their rescue, and that the more it spent, the better their chances of making a living.

By 1939—the year when World War II broke out—the gross public debt had increased from 24 billion dollars in 1933 to 47.6 billion dollars. The gross national product during the same period, if reckoned in 1939 dollars, grew from 61.5 billion dollars to 93.3 billion dollars. And gross private domestic investment (in 1939 dollars) increased from 1.6 billion dollars in 1933 to 9.9 billion dollars in 1939. Civilian employment increased from 38,760,000 in 1933 to 45,750,000 in 1939.

The only recession during that period—a rather sharp one in 1938—was preceded by a decline in government spending and a restrictive credit policy adopted by the Federal Reserve authorities because they feared inflation.

The percentage of the civilian labor force unemployed was 24.9 per cent in 1933 and 17.2 per cent in 1939. There were still 9,480,000 unemployed. But thereafter government had to spend even greater sums in preparing for war and fighting it.

Unemployment rapidly dropped to an absolute minimum; shortages of labor were prevalent.

This wide range of bad fortune and good, within a single lifetime, made a deep impression on the rank and file of the people. And only the dullest could fail to note the important effects which governmental policy exerted on their lives.

Even if Keynes were wholly wrong and the classical economists were right, that a competitive system would reach equilibrium at full employment if left alone, our system has so many approaches to monopoly and so many "administered" prices that the classical theory is almost as irrelevant as if it concerned another planet.

Business combinations and the control of prices and output through pools and gentlemen's agreements flourished after the Civil War. By 1904 the so-called trusts controlled 40 per cent of the manufacturing capital in the United States. Virtual monopoly control existed in thirty products, from asphalt to whisky, including electrical equipment, leather, petroleum products, glass, shoe machinery, steel, sugar, and tobacco. Anti-trust legislation and financial crises retarded, but did not destroy, the tendency toward concentration. It is estimated by Gardiner C. Means that in 1909 the two hundred largest nonfinancial corporations owned one-third of the business assets of the country (excluding banks, insurance companies, and other financial agencies).

During World War I big business grew rapidly because war contracts went mainly to the great concerns, and these concerns made huge profits, a large portion of which they laid aside for future expansion. Their reserves enabled most of them to weather the storm of 1921. The giant business concerns increased in importance during the 1920s, and mergers continued.

The two hundred largest nonfinancial corporations, which controlled one-third of the business assets in 1909, had 48 per cent in 1929. Their percentage of the total corporate income grew from 33 in 1920 to 43 in 1929. Five per cent of corporations earned 78.9 per cent of the corporate income of the country in 1918 and increased their share until it reached 87.9 per cent in 1932. Those manufacturing corporations, each of which had an annual net income of 5 million dollars or more, got 34.2 per cent of corporate manufacturing income in 1918 and 46.1 per cent in 1929. Those companies with annual net incomes of less than $250,000 lost ground, receiving 23.4 per cent of the total in manufacturing in 1918 and 19.1 per cent in 1929.

During the Great Depression all business suffered, and big business especially lost ground, because it exerts more control in the industries making capital goods, which decline more when business is bad. During the recovery, however, the tendency toward concentration made up for lost time. The 316 largest manufacturers held 35 per cent of the working capital in 1926 and 47 per cent in 1938. Manufacturing corporations, each having more than 50 million dollars in assets, owned 37 per cent of the total manufacturing assets in 1934 and 49 per cent in 1942. There were 205 of these giants in the latter year. In 1942 the manufacturing corporations, each of which received annual net income of 5 million dollars or more, had just over half the total manufacturing income, as compared with 46 per cent in 1929. On the other hand, manufacturing corporations with incomes of less than $250,000, which had received 19.1 per cent of the total income in 1929, had only 11.6 per cent in 1942.

In industries accounting for one-third the value of all American manufactured products, the four largest producers in each industry turned out more than three-fourths of the product of that industry.

The growth of big business under Franklin D. Roosevelt was primarily due not to combinations or mergers of separate companies but rather to expansion of individual concerns. Mergers, however, had thrived between 1919 and 1929. They were particularly numerous in iron and steel, machinery, producers of food, motion pictures, retail trade, and hotels. The concentration of holding-company control in electric power was notorious.

There were nearly three times as many mergers in 1929 as in 1919. During the depression and the subsequent New Deal recovery, the number of business consolidations fell off sharply. Concentration then became a matter of the growth of existing large companies.

The two hundred and fifty largest manufacturing corporations owned 65 per cent of the nation's production facilities in 1939. During the war they operated 79 per cent of all the new facilities built with federal funds and privately operated. They held options to purchase everything they operated.

About 26 billion dollars was spent during the war for new productive equipment—plants and machinery. Total manufacturing facilities existing in 1939 had cost 40 billion dollars. The new facilities were of the most modern design and the greatest efficiency. It is estimated that about 20 billion dollars' worth of the new capacity was usable for peacetime products. Nearly three-quarters of the outlay was to enlarge manufacture of the same product which the operator made before the war. Of more than a hundred thousand machine tools provided, 78 per cent were general-purpose tools.

Technological improvements and know-how, which make possible new types of products and cut costs of production, were developed during the war principally by the big companies. Research, much of it financed by the government, was conducted mainly in their laboratories. Out of war earnings, they spent millions to advertise their names and trademarks. After the end of the war the net working capital of the sixty-three largest manufacturing corporations was larger than that of all other manufacturing corporations listed with the Securities and Exchange Commission in 1939, or about 10 billion dollars.

Of the 175 billion dollars of prime government contracts awarded between June 1940 and October 1, 1944, nearly two-thirds went to the one hundred corporations which received the largest orders. More than half of the plums were awarded to only thirty-three companies, each of which had orders totaling a billion dollars or more. The first ten corporations received 30 per cent of the contract awards (by value).

At the top stood the General Motors Corporation with 13,812 million dollars of war orders. Other motor and plane companies were near the top of the list, which as a whole includes great corporations in many industries.

Did the big concerns share this business with the smaller ones by handing out subcontracts? Only slightly over one-third of the value of the prime contracts was passed on to subcontractors. Of this amount, approximately 75 per cent went to other large companies. These in turn made some further subcontracts. In the end, however, according to an estimate by the Smaller War Plants Corporation, the war production of small concerns amounted to only 30 per cent of the total.

The fact that a high degree of industrial concentration exists does not mean that there are not still many small businesses. In manufacturing, 98.9 per cent of the firms had in 1939 fewer than five hundred employees each. These firms employed 51.7 per cent of the factory workers. The effect of the war on small business is shown clearly by the fact that in 1944 the firms employing fewer than five hundred apiece, which still made up 97.8 per cent of all manufacturers, employed only 38.1 per cent of the factory workers. This shrinkage was particularly marked in the war industries. In the nonwar industries less change was noticed.

Those small businesses which succeeded in obtaining subcontracts became dependent on the large concerns for their sales and materials.

The big companies have been using their huge liquid assets to buy government facilities and smaller private concerns. After 1943 the rate of mergers and acquisitions was higher than in the previous fifteen years and shot up almost perpendicularly. Iron and steel and machinery accounted for 25 per cent of the total acquisitions between 1940 and 1945. Food and liquor, drugs and pharmaceuticals, also have become more highly concentrated.

Prices Are Administered

One must not conclude that the big concerns never compete with one another, or that all prices are set by monopolies. There obviously is competition in the automobile industry, for instance. But the competition is of a different sort from that which the classical economists had in mind. The big producer has the power to set his price and maintain it for a considerable period. He knows what the others in his field are likely to do; the interaction of this knowledge usually prevents much price-slashing. What is more likely to happen, if high prices reduce demand, is a cut in production and employment.

On the other hand, it will not do to underestimate the extent of monopoly price-fixing. In a study of cartels for the Twentieth Century Fund—*Cartels in Action* by George W. Stocking and Myron W. Atkins—the authors estimated that of 1939 sales in the United States, 87 per cent, by value, of mineral products, 60 per cent of agricultural products, and 42 per cent of manufactured products were cartelized.

Concentrated control is not, of course, all on the side of business. Labor organization has gained immense power to affect wages and hours through collective bargaining. This may be as just as it is inevitable under modern conditions, but it certainly does not lead to flexibility of wages or to competition in the labor market. Minimum wages enforced by government cover unorganized trades. Farmers, who normally would illustrate the classical effect of competition on prices, are now safeguarded by price supports and governmental payments of numerous kinds, and some system of the sort is likely to continue. Government agencies directly or indirectly control prices for transportation, power, and other services.

In these circumstances nobody can ever prove whether the classical economists were right in alleging that everything would automatically work out for the best under laissez faire. We don't have it; we haven't had it at least for a century; we are not going to have it in the visible future. The hard facts make the argument irrelevant. It is, of course, still possible that the prevalence of inflexibilities of prices and costs does lead to the changes in total demand which we know exist. But in that case the remedy is not to recommend a nonexistent and impossible noninterference. We must look for improvement in another direction. It must include planning and policy of some sort; it must hinge on decisions about prices and production made by those who have power to make them. The right decisions, we may assume as a working hypothesis, could lead to the equilibrium on a high level which traditional theory supposed would automatically result without planning. The task for social scientists is to discover what those right decisions are and how people can be induced to make them.

EIGHT

PLANNING FOR EMPLOYMENT

When World War II came to an end in 1945, the memory of large and stubbornly persistent unemployment in the 1930s was still fresh. It was obvious to all concerned—not merely to specialists in economics—that although the recovery which had begun in 1933 had increased production, incomes, and the number employed, there had occurred another brief but sharp recession in 1938, and that what really had pulled the national economy out of the doldrums was the immense demand for military goods and manpower financed by the federal government during World War II. Now, in the late 1940s, that demand was being rapidly diminished. One group of economists expected widespread unemployment as a result. Others thought that consumers' demands for goods which had been in short supply during the war, such as automobiles and housing, would exceed the supply as business producers struggled to reconvert to peacetime products, and that the immediate danger was rather that of inflation, with its rising prices.

There was, however, widespread agreement that, whatever the outcome, the economic policy of the federal government constituted a powerful influence on the course of the private-enterprise sector of the economy, in peace as well as in war, that the existence of this power involved a corresponding responsibility, and consequently that the government ought to acknowledge its duty and continuously plan to coordinate and use its power for the benefit of the citizens. No longer could government be regarded as an isolated activity which must be kept completely separate from a supposedly self-balancing and self-regulated private-enterprise economy. It was high time to abandon that ancient superstition.

Government's Pressure on Business

Government has long exerted many kinds of pressure on business, both direct and indirect. An old endeavor by government is to attempt to dissolve monopolies and force business to compete. Though successful in some respects, this policy has done little to prevent the growth of industrial concentration. Government has also had a finger in the regulation of rates and prices, particularly in railroads and public utilities. It has prescribed the methods and standards of labor policy. During emergencies its regulation has extended over a much wider field. Its taxation laws and rulings have had a profound effect on business decisions. These are only the more important types of governmental intervention.

Part of the lack of public standards for industrial management has arisen from the confused effect of governmental pressure taken as a whole. During war the confusion is lessened, though the pressure is greatly increased. War necessities put before the nation certain major objectives, such as increased production of munitions and food and the direction of resources and manpower into the most essential uses. Big business has had signal success in adjusting its activities to the national effort under these circumstances. Though in detail the record is spotty, the general achievement is attested by the remarkable increases of war production. But in peace, managers have often been at a loss to know what they lawfully could do or not do in respect to competition, trade practices, collective bargaining, accounting, tax payment, and so on. Their usual effort has been, under ordinary circumstances, to try to avoid getting into trouble with the law while pursuing whatever course happened to seem advisable at the time, rather than to cooperate for positive purposes in a national program.

Among economists there are various schools of thought about what attitude toward business should be adopted by government. As far as business organization is concerned, there are three main doctrines. The first is the one traditional in this country, that government should force business to compete. Once it has done that, these economists believe, competition itself will see that business serves the public welfare. Regulation is of course permissible to soften the extreme rigors of competition where it is most severe—as in agriculture or the labor market. Regulation or public ownership is also required where monopoly is unavoidable in essential public services—as in railroads or utilities. Beyond this, however, the goal is "free, competitive private enterprise," enforced by government.

A small (in the United States) but persistent minority holds to the theory that private enterprise will not in most instances serve the public welfare and that the solution lies in the direction of socialism. Public or cooperative ownership is advocated at least for important or basic industries; some would go further than that.

The doctrines emphasized by Keynes may be combined with either of these attitudes toward business organization. It is possible to hold that the government can, and should, compensate for irregularities of employment by its own policies of spending and taxing, and at the same time to believe in letting businesses run themselves so long as they compete. It is equally possible to argue that the whole difficulty would be avoided if the government itself regularly made most of the decisions about business investment, prices, and production, as it would if it owned industry.

A third general point of view about business does not place its emphasis upon either governmental policing of business or governmental ownership. No matter what form business management has or may take, this school stresses something new—the choice of a peacetime goal, the working out of definite policies to approach that goal, and the cooperation of government, business, labor, and agriculture in the attempt to apply those policies. Implicit in this attitude is the assumption that business managers have much discretion to decide about prices, volume of investment, and the like, that it is possible to work out guides for these decisions which will accord with the public welfare, and that business managers, as well as labor and farm leaders, can in fact cooperate with the government in seeking the declared goal. At least it is desirable, according to this view, to work out coherent standards for decisions and to give industrial managers the opportunity to cooperate before trying more drastic methods.

The Employment Act and the Economic Council

In 1946 Congress passed the Employment Act, which set a leading economic objective for the country, though it did not mention specific immediate goals, and established an official agency and procedures to seek the objective. The objective is the maintenance of a high level of employment and production. This law was inspired partly by those who wanted a governmental fiscal policy to compensate for the ups and downs of demand originating in the operations of private business, and partly by those who believed in trying to enlist the cooperation of business in stabilizing the economy.

The main policy is defined in the law as follows:

> The Congress hereby declares that it is the continuing policy and responsibility of the Federal Government to use all practicable means consistent with its needs and obligations and other essential considerations of national policy, with the assistance and cooperation of industry, agriculture, labor, and State and local governments, to coordinate and utilize all its plans, functions, and resources for the purpose of creating and maintaining, in a manner calculated to foster and promote free competitive enterprise and the general welfare, conditions under which there will be afforded useful employment opportunities, including self employment, to those able, willing and seeking to work, and to promote maximum employment, production and purchasing power.

Under this law the President must submit to Congress at the beginning of each session an economic report reviewing the existing economic situation and the trends, stating the level of employment, production, and purchasing power needed to carry out the declared policy, and containing a program for carrying out the policy, together with recommendations for any desirable legislation. Supplementary economic reports may be made during the year.

Congress has established a joint committee from the House and Senate to review this report. The committee is bound by law to state its position on the recommendations of the President and to sponsor bills carrying out any suggestions which it approves.

The Economic Reports of the President are prepared with the advice of an expert Council of Economic Advisers consisting of three men with a relatively small staff. This council is part of the Executive Office and is directly under the President. It consults with business, labor, agriculture, and consumer organizations in the course of formulating and carrying out the policy of the law.

The enormous statistical resources of the government are available to the council. Its reports have constituted the most comprehensive picture of the contemporary economic situation ever made available to the officials and people of the country, and have contained the first regular official economic programs aimed at achieving a leading objective defined by law.

The nation is now equipped, therefore, with a series of economic instruments, most of which it never had before the end of World War II. It has:

1. An enormous amount of current statistics which, when pieced together correctly, give a revealing picture of the existing situation.
2. A declared economic objective for peacetime, embodied in law by Congress: maximum employment, production, and purchasing power.
3. A legally authorized body of experts, in the office of the Chief Executive, to interpret the facts and tell us what ought to be done to seek the objective.
4. A major committee of Congress to study the Economic Report of the President and recommend legislation.
5. A legal authorization for the expert advisers of the President to enlist the cooperation of business, agriculture, labor, and state and local governments in seeking this end.

This was a good beginning. There remained, however, the formidable task of developing an accurate and meaningful understanding of the economic situation at the time, valid recommendations as to what should be done about it, and acceptance of these policies by those having power to make decisions about action. Our understanding of this task may be illuminated by examining how the Economic Council actually did analyze the situation in the first annual Economic Report of the President, issued in January 1947. Its over-all picture of the situation—based on national-income accounting—was contained in a table entitled "The Nation's Economic Budget."

The Nation's Economic Budget

Everyone is familiar with budgets of one kind or another—household budgets, business budgets, the budget of the federal government. This new one was a super-budget, covering the activities of the whole national economy—individuals, business, and government. "The Nation's Economic Budget" could not have been constructed without the work which has gone into understanding and recording the national income. For, like all the budgets for smaller units, it is a matter of matching income against spending.

But there is one important difference between this budget and all the others. A housewife or a businessman, when working out a budget, is concerned mainly with the struggle to make income cover expenses. The aim is to keep income up and expenses down, so that there shall be no deficit and, if possible, a surplus. In the nation's economic budget, however, there cannot possibly be either a deficit or a surplus. Income will necessarily, and without effort on anybody's part, exactly match outgo. If any difference is shown between receipts and expenditures, the economist knows that there is something wrong with the figures. He examines the statistics to find the error. To achieve a balance is merely a matter of checking the accuracy of the calculations; it is not the purpose of drawing up the budget.

This balance is a fundamental equation of economics, like the basic equations of any other science. It is axiomatic. If only an individual were concerned, his income would probably be less or greater than his outgo. The same is true of a business, or of any part of the total economy, such as an industry or the federal government. But if all individuals, all businesses, and all other economic units are taken into account, their aggregate income must equal their outgo, since there is no way for any one of these units to receive income except as a result of equivalent expenditure by one or more of the others.

The purposes to which this equation may conceivably be put are many, but in 1947 there was concern chiefly with examining and forecasting the total of expenditure. What everybody spends constitutes the total demand. This demand in large part determines whether there will be inflation at one extreme or depression and unemployment at the other. It may be possible to predict the future of demand, or even to influence it, if the various units which contribute to the total can be properly classified and their contribution to demand measured.

The Flow of Income

In order to understand this budget, it is necessary to bear in mind the flow of money about the system. Everybody receives money; everybody pays it out. Table 6 measures this flow at several important gates.

TABLE 6. THE NATION'S ECONOMIC BUDGET, 1946[1]

(*Billions of Dollars*)

Accounts	*Receipts*	*Expenditures*	*Excess (+) or Deficit (−)*
Consumers:			
Disposable income	158.4		
Expenditures		143.7	
Saving (+)			+14.8
Business:			
Undistributed profits and reserves	13.3		
Gross domestic investment:			
New construction		8.5	
Producers' durable equipment		12.4	
Changes in inventories		3.7	
Total		24.6	
Excess of receipts (+) or investment (−)			−11.3
International:			
Net foreign investment		4.8	
Excess of receipts (+) or investment (−)			−4.8
Government (federal, state, and local):			
Cash receipts from the public	56.5		
Cash payments to the public		55.2	
Excess of receipts (+) or payments (−)			+1.3
			0

[1] From the Economic Report of the President, January 1947.

(The careful reader need not be disturbed by the fact that the column for receipts adds up to 228.2, while the column for expenditures adds up to 228.3. This is merely the result of rounding out the decimals—that is, if any decimal, carried out further, is less than .5 larger, the excess is ignored, whereas if the excess is more than .5, 1 is added to the final column.)

It is both convenient and logical to start measuring with consumers, since that classification includes every living soul and much of the money flow pours through this gate. We want to measure, first, the purchasing power going to consumers and see what they do with it. Their "disposable income" was 158.4 billion dollars. This means all the money they could possibly spend. Technically, consumers' income was larger than this, since it included money paid out for taxes to the government and other obligatory contributions. But these are here accounted for under other headings. Of consumers' disposable income, they spent 143.7 billion dollars and saved, that is, did not spend, 14.8 billion dollars.

What consumers spend is received largely by business (including, of course, agriculture and professional men). Since we have accounted already for consumers' spending, it would be duplication to set it down again at the gate of business income. Only that part of business income which business does not pay back again, directly or indirectly to individuals, must be listed as business receipts. These undistributed profits and reserves amounted to 13.3 billion dollars.

What does business spend, outside of the payments for current services, dividends, and so forth? The remaining expenditure is for what is ordinarily called "capital" goods. New construction accounted for 8.5 billion dollars. This includes factories, railroads, commercial and industrial construction of all types. It also includes residential buildings. Most residential construction projects are undertaken by business concerns; those houses built by people who expect to occupy them are lumped with the rest for convenience. Producers' durable equipment—machinery and the like—took 12.4 billion dollars. Finally, business may enlarge or diminish its stock of goods. In this case, the inventories were enlarged by 3.7 billion dollars. This figure covers only goods actually added to inventories. Revaluation of existing stocks of goods due to price changes is excluded, since that is not part of the money flow; it is merely a change in bookkeeping figures.

Altogether, business spent, for investment purposes, 24.6 billion dollars, or 11.3 billion more than it received as undistributed income. Of course this does not mean that it operated at a loss. Business made tremendous profits in 1946. The deficit in this table merely reflects the fact that business invested other people's money, which is obtained by borrowing it or by selling shares. This investment goes into the same column in which is listed the surplus which consumers did not spend but saved. Part of the consumers' surplus was used to buy the mortgages, bonds, or stocks by the sale of which business obtained the extra money to invest.

Part of the saved money flowed abroad rather than into spending or investment in this country. That part of the flow is measured at the gate called "International." Here we are not concerned with everything spent abroad, or everything contributed to our income by foreigners, but only with the difference between these two totals. We made available for the use of foreigners 4.8 billion dollars more than they made available for our use. Under normal circumstances this sum would constitute an increase of their debt to us; hence it is called an investment. Actually much of it was given away in 1946, but it must nevertheless be put down in the table, since the money must be accounted for.

Last of all is the gate of government. Here is put down *all* the money which was received by governmental units in this country and all the money they spent. This involves no duplication, since taxes and other payments to government by consumers have been omitted in listing their disposable income, and business taxes are deducted before undistributed profits are reckoned.

Government took in 56.5 billion dollars; it spent 55.2 billion. Thus there was a surplus of 1.3 billion dollars to carry over into the last column.

What government spent went in part directly to consumers as wages and salaries. In part, it went to pay business for products and services; much of this sum business paid out again to consumers, and the rest turned up in undistributed profits.

Now look at the right-hand column containing the excess or deficit of expenditure for each main item. It will be seen that they exactly balance out; the total of the column is zero. Individual consumers and government spent less than they received; this surplus or "saving" was used partly to increase domestic business investment, partly to increase foreign investment.

It should be noted, by the way, that not all the investment is included in the right-hand column. Before the excess of business expenditures over receipts was reckoned and carried across to the last column, business was recorded as spending 13.3 billion dollars of its own accumulations. Taking account of this, the total number of dollars spent for investment was 29.4 billion, rather than 16.1 billion. Exactly the same amount was saved. In such a tabulation, saving must always equal investment.

Using the Budget

At the beginning of 1947, when these figures were compiled, nearly everyone was concerned with curbing inflation—that is, halting a rapid general rise of prices. How was this to be done? The main object was to prevent the total demand from growing. While some people had too little to spend, and many others would have been glad to enlarge their own incomes, a greater aggregate income would be almost sure to result in higher prices.

Here the amount of production enters the calculation. Money is spent for goods and services. If the output of these could be increased, expenditures could be enlarged by the same percentage without boosting prices. But there is a limit to the gain of production in a given time and with a given amount of work. In 1946 there had been no important reservoir of unemployed to call upon. To be sure, there had been big strikes, hence fewer labor disputes would mean more labor hours. Efficiency, too, might advance somewhat as new machinery was installed and people became accustomed to their new jobs. But a good estimate made by economists at the beginning of 1947 was that total output for that year might be about 5 per cent larger than in 1946—scarcely greater. No matter how much was spent, people could not buy any more goods than could be produced. It would be well, if possible, to keep total spending from growing at all, since in that case any gain in output could mean lower prices.

It is one of the elementary principles of economics, known to everybody, that when demand is greater than supply, prices tend to rise. In social accounting of the type represented by this budget, aggregate demand is total expenditure. These are just different names for the same thing. And one would not even have to know the elementary law of demand and supply to understand that if more money were spent for the same amount of goods, the price of the goods must be higher. That is an arithmetical necessity. If I pay $60 for two suits of clothes, the average price of the suit is $30. If in the following year, I pay $80 for two suits, their average price is $40. It is as simple as that.

Now, then, let us look at the table to see where the pressure for higher prices came from. A great many people said it came from high wages. Many other people said it came from large profits to business or farmers. Still others said it came from foreign demand for American goods. The first fact to notice is that it came from all these things put together. Every spending group contributed to the demand.

Consumer expenditures were obviously larger than those of any other group. But not all consumer income came from wages. There are also lumped in the figure the income from dividends, rents, farms and unincorporated businesses, and interest on private investments. If we ignore for the moment the taxes deducted to reckon "disposable" income, rental income was 6.9 billion dollars, dividends, 5.6 billion dollars. If wages alone were kept from rising, some of these other items might grow enough to cancel the restrictions.

Nevertheless, one of the most important gates at which to control the flow of spending was that of consumers. One obvious way to keep this gate from opening wider might have been to impose price-control. For if consumers did not pay more for each unit, their spending could not increase, unless there should be more goods to buy. But suppose their incomes did increase. What would they do with the extra money? Clearly, they would have to save it. And, in that case, it would probably be invested at home (that is, spent for capital goods) or invested or given abroad, thus increasing the spending of foreigners. Even aside from black markets which may make price-control more or less ineffectual, incomes as well as consumer spending must be limited if total demand is to be limited. Therefore, it would have been necessary not only to have price-control, but to limit rises of wages and salaries and to control rents.

How about limiting business income? Well, if price-control could be enforced, business profits would be limited almost automatically. Business income as a whole was determined by two factors: (1) the number of things it had for sale; and (2) the prices at which they were sold. It could not get many more things to sell; therefore, if prices were prevented from rising, it could not make much larger profits—unless it paid less for labor, in which case labor income would shrink by a compensating amount. Freezing of prices of farm products would likewise keep farmers' profits from growing.

Price-control had been, in fact, abandoned in 1946. But in 1947 business was urged not to raise its prices; labor was urged to go slow on wage increases. When some wage increases were made, business was advised to absorb the extra cost, either by greater efficiency, which would release labor for more production, or by accepting smaller profits.

How about limiting foreign spending in this country? That

would have helped a little to control inflation, but the net foreign demand was so small in relation to the total demand that it could not have helped much. And for other reasons it was not wise to cut this item of expenditure.

Finally, we come to government spending. This is a tricky item, and many people have misunderstood its effect. A popular slogan has been "cut government spending—here is where the pressure for inflation arises!" But remember that when government has a balanced budget or a surplus, most of the money it spends is raised by taxes or other contributions which individuals or business have to pay, and which consequently reduce *their* spending. Cutting taxes in these circumstances would merely give consumers and business more to spend. It would probably not reduce total spending by one cent.

If government reduced its spending *without* lowering taxes, that would help. The critical item here is the *difference* between government receipts and expenditures, that is, the cash surplus.

What happens to such a governmental surplus? It may be loaned abroad, in which case it increases demand. It may be used to pay off government bonds in the hands of individual citizens or business concerns, in which case they can invest or spend what they receive from the government. But it *may* be used to retire government securities in the hands of the banks, in which case the money may be made to disappear into thin air by action of the Federal Reserve authorities. This is one of the mysteries of the banking system, which has been explained in a previous chapter. To maintain a sizable government excess of receipts over expenditures is one of the best ways to fight inflation. The government thus takes money from the people which it does not give back; then it can wave a wand and, presto! the money is gone.

What Happened in 1947

As many people will remember, inflation was decidedly not curbed in 1947 but took a new lease of life. This was particularly true in the latter six months of the year. The gate of price-control was not closed, and admonitions to keep prices down voluntarily were not very successful. There were wage increases, and the pressure of foreign demand also grew. Meanwhile production increased only about 5 per cent, as predicted. The annual rates at which the various important economic groups were receiving and spending money in the second half of 1947 as compared with 1946 were as follows:

Consumers' disposable income rose to 180.8 billion dollars from 158.4 billion in 1946.
Of this, consumers spent 169 billion dollars instead of 143.7 billion as in 1946.

Business surplus income rose to 17.8 billion dollars from 13.3 billion.
Business investment was 31.7 billion dollars instead of 24.6 billion.

Net foreign investment was 8.2 billion dollars instead of 4.8 billion.

Government received from the public 58.7 billion dollars instead of 56.5 billion.
Government payments to the public *fell* to 52.7 billion dollars from 55.2 billion.

There is a particularly noteworthy fact about these changes. Government expenditures, alone among all the items, decreased. At the same time, government receipts increased slightly. Government was therefore the only factor which exerted an influence to reduce demand and hence to curb inflation. Here was a gate which shut a little way against the money flow. This result was made possible because taxes were not reduced. If they had been, consumers' disposable income and business income would have been correspondingly increased, and the reduction of government spending would probably have been without effect in limiting total demand.

It is also interesting that the difference between what consumers received and what they spent was narrowing. Their current savings shrank from 14.8 billion dollars in 1946 to an annual rate of 11.8 billion dollars in the last half of 1947. The increase of investment which occurred was financed not out of larger savings by individuals, but out of larger undistributed profits.

How far could this tendency go? Certainly the time might come when consumers, pressed hard by high prices, would cease to cut their savings and start to cut their purchases instead. Then business profits would quickly feel the effect, and business would invest less. With both consumers and business spending less, total demand would fall. If the fall continued, it could readily bring depression and unemployment unless government quickly reversed its fiscal policy and started to spend more than it received. Note that this conclusion is based not on a vague theory of "deficit spending," but on an inspection of actual figures of spending.

Comparison with Prewar

Everybody knows that both national income and spending were much greater after the war than before it. But it is interesting to see actual figures for the main groups of spenders. These figures have been calculated so as to eliminate the effect of price increases. They indicate roughly the change in the actual quantities bought.

Consumers bought in 1947 about 48 per cent more than in 1939.

New business investment in 1947 was about 170 per cent more than in 1939.

There was an even larger percentage increase in "net foreign investment," but this item started at such a low level in 1939 that it did not make nearly as much difference as the other two.

Government before the war had a deficit; after the war it had a surplus. Therefore no percentage comparison is possible; but it was not making a net contribution to demand in 1947, as it did in 1939.

Whatever may be the nation's need for new capital, it can be said that in 1947 we were piling it up much more rapidly than before the war. The inflationary pressure resulting from expanded business investment was much sharper than that resulting from increased consumer buying. The same tendency continued in 1948.

Even if consumers did not start to buy less because of high prices, business might come to the end of its postwar investment program. Then business spending for new investment would shrink. This shrinkage might conceivably be just enough to stop inflation. But if it went beyond that, unemployment would grow, unless more spending from some other quarter (presumably government) counterbalanced the shrinkage.

The great value of the kind of thinking that developed the nation's economic budget is that it makes possible consideration of such possibilities *before they happen*. Thus it is an instrument which can be used to forestall either inflation or unemployment if all the people who make decisions about spending, setting wages or prices, saving, and investment understand it properly and will consent to take the appropriate action.

Nevertheless, in 1947 at least one essential element in carrying out such a policy was lacking—ability to make reasonably accurate forecasts of the course of the business cycle. As we have previously seen (Chapter 5), this advance was not achieved until about ten years later. In January 1948 the Council of Economic Advisers recommended, and President Truman supported, maintaining a surplus in the federal budget, in order to check the current inflationary rise in prices. Neither expected an imminent recession. Congress, however, ignored this advice by reducing taxes, in response to pressure from business and individual taxpayers, and even reversed the President's veto of the tax bill. Late in 1948, a moderate recession began, and the budgetary deficit of 1949, caused largely by tax reduction, helped to dampen it. Thus, for the wrong reasons, Congress helped to moderate a recession by ignoring the advice of a President and his Economic Council, who, for the right reasons but without sufficient knowledge of the behavior of the economy. had recommended the wrong action.

Increasing the National Income

The process of planning for employment undertaken by the President's Economic Council had not gone very far when they added to their objective of moderating cyclical unemployment and inflation the aim of facilitating long-term increase in the national income—assuredly authorized in the phrases of the Employment Act which made it a "responsibility of the Federal Government ... to promote maximum ... production." This aim of favoring increased production over the long term has later come to be known as a policy for "economic growth."

During the depression of the 1930s the prevailing opinion was that private business must and will pursue its incalculable way, and that the most government could do would be to compensate for its vagaries. When war brought prosperity of its own kind, attention was shifted to avoiding the depression which experience had shown was likely to follow it. More recently, another attitude has been gaining ground. It might be possible, it even might be practical and effective, to substitute for these negative views a positive program. Instead of asking how a depression could be avoided or compensated for, once it had arrived, we could lay out a program for producing whatever the nation most needed and then try to keep production high in gaining these goals. We know that needs here and in the rest of the world are far greater than the utmost possible total of production can satisfy. Depression would necessarily be avoided if only we could keep busy making and distributing urgently required goods and services. Not anti-depression measures, but pro-production measures, may yield the greatest benefit.

The Council of Economic Advisers, in drafting the Economic Reports of the President, began concretely to outline objectives of this kind and to indicate what measures are necessary to achieve them. In the report for January 1948 it surveyed briefly the possibilities of increased income in the future and the means of enlarging production. It estimated conservatively that ten years hence there could be a per-capita disposable income "about 80 per cent above the level of 1937 and 27 per cent above the level of 1947 in terms of constant dollars. . . . We have within our reach an economic environment that would make it unnecessary for masses of people to be undernourished or ill-housed, to work in obsolete plants or shops, or to lack essential medical care, social security, or education."

The report discussed our resources of land, water, forests, minerals, and what should be done to preserve and make more efficient use of them. It indicated what was required to increase industrial capacity so that there might be an efficient balance among industries. It outlined needed effort and expenditure in transportation, urban development, housing, education, health, old-age security. It then discussed more general policies adapted to achieving long-term goals.

This was merely a beginning. The pointing out of possibilities or needs, and the discussion of policies, is a long way from assuring that all concerned will take the required action. It was a great advance, however, that now for the first time all these subjects could be discussed not as vague abstractions but in the setting of fairly accurate knowledge of what it is physically possible to produce and what our income looks like. Economic science has at last begun to give us the mental tools by the use of which national economic policy can be something better than an expression of prejudice and something more substantial than a daydream.

Parenthetically, the estimate of the council made in January 1948, that within ten years per-capita disposable income in the United States might increase 27 per cent in constant dollars (that is, after accounting for changes in the "cost of living" or consumers' prices), turned out to be too high. If you divide all the disposable income received by individuals in the United States in 1947 by the number of these individuals, you will get (in dollars that would buy as much as in 1962) $1560 per person. In 1957, the same calculation turned out an average income of $1919. The percentage increase was 20 per cent for the decade, not 27 per cent.

The actual record of the business cycle and of economic growth since 1945 is discussed in Chapters 9 and 10.

The Great Unanswered Question

Knowledge, it has been said, is power. Power, however, has to be picked up and used if it is to achieve anything, and it must be used for good ends if it is not to be destructive. We still do not know whether the kind of society we have is capable of making the best use of the new science of economics. Will those who must make decisions pay sufficient attention to the organized facts? Will they accept as criteria for action the standards which the new knowledge has begun to provide? We do not know.

Some have already made up their minds that the hope is vain. Private enterprise, perhaps even human nature itself, they are sure, is not equal to the test. Too many special interests, too many group pressures, are at work. These pessimists may be right, but it is necessary to point out that there was little scientific evidence for their gloomy conclusion, since the test had never before been made except in major wars. We cannot tell what people are capable of until they are provided with the knowledge and the standards which would enable them to know what they ought to do. The rudiments of this knowledge are now available to Americans for the first time in their history. The first experiment in enlightened and voluntary economic government is at hand. Democracy has already proved its compatibility with great achievements in detailed management of industry and agriculture. Perhaps the fate of the world for centuries to come depends now on the capacity of democracy to do a creditable job in management of the economy as a whole.

In the first place, it must be understood that the Economic Council is a council of *advisers*. It has no direct power to put into practice any policy which it may recommend. It is only one of the agencies advising the chief executive of the nation.

The President is also advised by his Cabinet members, all of whom administer departments which must have, in one field or another, important economic policies. (The Department of Defense is an outstanding example.) He is advised by the Budget Bureau, which may have even greater power than the Secretary of the Treasury in deciding what expenditures are to be recommended, what taxes Congress is to be asked to assess, and what the fiscal policy of the government is to be. The so-called independent agencies, such as the Board of Governors of the Federal Reserve System, the Federal Trade Commission, or the Interstate Commerce Commission are closely associated with important economic decisions in their several fields of responsibility—banks, money and credit, business trade practices, and interstate transportation. There are commissions or administrations concerned with shipping, air transport, power, radio and television, subsidized housing, securities and stock exchanges. If the main recommendations of the Economic Council are to influence the action of the President, it must also help in some way to coordinate the aims and methods of such executive agencies. The President, of course, has the power and the responsibility to see that the part of government which he controls does follow a consistent and effective general program, and he should be greatly assisted in doing so because the Council of Economic Advisers presents a reasonably accurate and meaningful account of the state of the national economy as a whole.

The President, however, is not constitutionally in a position to act—except in emergencies or as Commander-in-Chief of the armed forces—unless the legislative branch of our "system of checks and balances" has granted or will grant him the necessary statutes, appropriations, and tax legislation. Calling signals for the team of executive agencies is child's play compared with obtaining—and obtaining promptly enough—passage of the necessary measures by Congress. The agency to facilitate this outcome, established by the Employment Act of 1946, is the Joint Economic Committee, consisting of members from both houses of our bicameral legislative body. This committee has been ably staffed. It has held many excellent hearings based on the President's Economic Report and has issued many informative reports of its own. Presumably it has played an important role in the economic education of senators and members of Congress, and of influential citizens. Nevertheless, as political scientists have repeatedly pointed out, the party system of the nation and the legislative process are so beset by inconsistencies and pitfalls that, except in great national emergencies, some Presidential recommendations to the Congress are likely to be defeated, greatly modified, or at best accepted only after long delay.

Each of the two major parties contains both liberals and conservatives. Senators and representatives may, and frequently do, oppose measures recommended by a President who is supposed to be the leader of their own party. Many place interests of their localities above the interests of the nation. Many are swayed by lobbyists representing powerful special interests, who control important contributions to election campaigns or blocs of votes. All legislative proposals must, before submission to the votes of the legislators, pass through Congressional committees, the powerful chairmen of which owe their positions not to their knowledge or ability but to the number of years they have been elected to Congress. This seniority system naturally favors the senators and representatives from regions where a single party almost always wins the elections—as in the Southern states. The Southern Democrats are usually conservative whereas the Northern Democrats are as a rule more liberal than the Northern Republicans. Presidential recommendations are frequently defeated, or delayed, by a Congressional coalition of Republicans and Democrats.

In the Senate, a stubborn minority may defeat a bill they dislike by a filibuster which prevents passage of any legislation until the majority surrenders, since the Senate rules allow members to talk as long as they like and do not require senators to confine their remarks to material relevant to the subject supposed to be the current business of the Senate. For many years, the apportionment of Congressional districts has given rural populations a larger representation than city dwellers. (This inequality may be remedied by a recent Supreme Court decision.)

To put the situation mildly, a legislative process of this kind is not likely to favor a national economy imposed on the people by a dictatorship which is guided by a rigid economic plan. Few Americans would regret that conclusion. But Congress might seem an effectual preventive of any sensible over-all economic planning at all. The outlook, however, is not so grim as it appears. There are, in the Congress as well as in the executive agencies, many able, well-educated, and public-spirited men. They are influenced by the needs of the nation as a whole, as well as by "practical politics." And it often is good practical politics to be associated, in the minds of the voters, with policies that serve the citizens as a whole rather than those that merely favor special interests. The Joint Economic Committee might enlarge its influence on current legislation if its advice were routinely asked during other committee hearings on any measure which involved economic policy.

The Council of Economic Advisers and its annual Economic Report are already known to many citizens who are concerned with the state of the nation. Such matters command the attention not only of professional economists but of bankers, business executives, labor leaders, and agencies of many kinds which are concerned with investment and markets. Indeed, professional economists are often consulted, or employed, by large business concerns, banks, labor and farmer organizations. Those familiar with the Economic Reports may not agree with their conclusions and recommendations, but at least most of the readers are interested in the same goals and in appropriate public policies.

This constituency in the public may reflect some economic light into the dim halls of Congressional procedure.

Can Private Enterprise Aid National Planning?

In classical economic thinking competitive, free private enterprise is completely incompatible with national economic planning. In a competitive economic order, every private economic activity depends on the interplay of prices and costs in free markets. Businessmen who seek their own profits benefit the general welfare more than if they deliberately tried to do so. They are guided "as if by an invisible hand" to serve public interest, as Adam Smith put it. Government, of course, may and should seek the general welfare in its own activities of taxing and spending, but it disobeys the classical "laws" if it either subsidizes or controls the private sector of the economy.

It is obvious that there does not now exist, either in the United States or anywhere else, an economic order which closely resembles competitive private enterprise as visualized by Adam Smith. What sort of order do we actually have, and may this order facilitate national economic policies applied not just to governmental taxing and spending but to the economy as a whole?

In their efforts to analyze the effects of business concentration, economic theorists have developed several new ideas. The old theory was content with expounding what would happen under the competition which it took for granted was characteristic of private enterprise, and, alternatively, what would happen under monopoly, which was the opposite of competition. One set of "laws" was supposed to govern prices, demand, and production under competition, another set concerned the behavior of monopoly. Both sets were deduced from what it was believed a businessman would do to gain the highest possible profit by selling a particular kind of article in a particular market.

But neither competition nor monopoly was very carefully defined. In actual economic life, there are all sorts of situations which differ from "perfect competition" on one side, and from complete monopoly on the other. Starting from the end of competition, economists began to discuss the changes of theory that would have to be made in the case of "imperfect competition"—that is, a situation in which, though competitive forces are at work, they operate slowly or incompletely. And starting from the end of complete monopoly, they worked back to "duopoly," where two producers dominate a market, or "oligopoly," where a few producers do so. Recently they have turned their attention to the situation where there is a monopoly or partial monopoly of buyers, as distinguished from sellers. The terms invented to describe this situation are "monopsony" (one buyer), "duopsony" (two buyers), "oligopsony" (a few buyers). Playing with these terms, the agile theorist can go on to chart what he supposes would happen when a monopoly confronts a monopsony, an oligopoly an oligopsony, and all the other possible permutations and combinations.

Administered Enterprise

All this is a fascinating game for those adept at it and may yield important conclusions. It is still, however, largely in the speculative stage which characterized the main body of classical theory before much statistical measurement became possible. Meanwhile, there is developing another approach to the subject which holds that the kind of economy we have does not work according to the theories of competition, on one hand, or of monopoly, on the other, and cannot be explained solely by a theory that there is a mixture of the two. A large part of industry is controlled by a type of organization which is a different sort of thing altogether and is not seeking primarily to maximize profit in the sales of a specific article in a specific market.

The great business organization, it is pointed out, is not today controlled by "owners"—that is, stockholders. It is governed by managers or executives who, though technically appointed by a board of directors who in turn are legally elected by stockholders, are in fact pretty much on their own, once they have gained high position. These managers, of course, have a responsibility to keep revenue above costs over the long run; in that sense they are concerned with profits. But in such an organization profit is usually a sort of by-product which results from a host of decisions about policy of many different kinds.

It is a leading aim of the manager to safeguard the future stability and growth of the enterprise, not just to make the largest possible profit on a particular transaction. He exercises a good deal of control over the cost of what he buys. He can enlarge the "cost" of operation by adopting one kind of treatment of depreciation, inventory valuation, and reserves; he can reduce it by another kind of treatment of these accounts. Profits can be taken in one year or projected into the future according to the type of accounting used. Indeed, it is common to have simultaneously at least two different sets of accounts, one to satisfy the income-tax authorities and another to satisfy the Securities and Exchange Commission and to make public.

Prices in turn are set not primarily by the competitive forces of the market, as the traditional economist understands it, but by decisions of the seller. This does not necessarily mean he sets the price to maximize profit on each given article. He may sell dozens of kinds of articles, some of them at no profit or a loss, others at a very high margin. He is governed by rules of thumb, custom, general policy for the future, considerations of prestige, desire to keep good will. He may control raw materials, semi-finished products, finished products; his operations may extend all the way to the consumer. He may take a profit at one point in this line and sacrifice it at another. Once a price structure is set, it has all sorts of interrelationships which are difficult to modify; nevertheless, it may have to be modified, both generally and in detail, because of technological changes, changes in "cost," changes in demand. The kind of price that is set by the seller in the hope that it will have some degree of permanency but that nevertheless will not be completely under his control, since conditions may force him to modify it, is not primarily either a competitive price or a monopoly price or any simple cross between the two. It is an "administered price."

The modern industrial manager has to make administrative decisions about things other than prices which have an important effect on the economy as a whole. Under the stress of collective bargaining, he decides about wages, hours of work, and other elements of labor cost. He decides how much of the net income shall be paid out in dividends, and how much shall be left in "retained earnings." He decides what new investment shall be made and when, how much of its cost shall be paid out of the corporation's own savings and how much by borrowing or selling securities. He decides the rate at which production or purchasing shall go on—a rate which is not necessarily parallel to the amount of sales. He decides, in other words, when to build up inventories and when to cut them down. The "industrial manager" does not necessarily mean a single dictator of a company's fortunes. Decisions of this sort arise out of advice, careful discussion, or even out of a body of rules and practices worked out with the aid of research and experience.

A book on this type of business published in 1948, *Managerial Enterprise,* is by Oswald W. Knauth, who had the advantage of both the training of a professional economist and extensive experience in business management of the new type. Mr. Knauth estimated that managerial enterprise controlled about half the production in the United States, the other half being divided between free enterprise of the old competitive kind and governmental or, as he called it, collective enterprise.

In Mr. Knauth's opinion, the manager is in reality a sort of mediator in behalf of the company as an institution. He mediates among the contending forces of owners, employees, customers, and government. His decisions affect the fortunes of all of them, the future of the corporation itself, and, of course, the general welfare of the country and the world. But this type of calling is comparatively recent and is not governed by any clear set of standards. The manager of a great concern usually has, for the time being, a wide margin of discretion in which to make his important choices without wrecking his enterprise. He has lost the old and clear imperatives of competition, yet nothing very definite has been substituted for them. He usually has ideas about the proper kind of industrial or public policy, though there is little assurance that in any given case these ideas are the best ones.

Organized Labor

As large industrial enterprises have assumed a leading role in the behavior of the economy, large and powerful labor organizations have developed, with the recognized function—under federal legislation—of protecting the interest of their members by collective bargaining. The decisions subject to such bargaining include wage rates, the standard work week, seniority in promotion, settlement of day-to-day disciplinary disputes, and numerous "fringe benefits" such as vacations, social insurance, pensions, and retirement policy. Labor leaders therefore have a power and a social responsibility which is parallel to that of the industrial manager in its effect on the economy as a whole.

The widespread growth of unions and collective bargaining has modified the nature of the national economy much as the great corporations have modified it. Both have greatly diminished the role of atomistic competition as conceived in the classical theory—management acting in the determination of prices and production, labor in the determination of wages and working conditions. The only rational kind of decision in either case consists of intelligent pursuit of sound economic policy for both—within the framework of a sound economy. Leaders on both sides of this market are deeply concerned with economic measures and decisions which must be made by government, just as governmental agencies are deeply concerned with the need to settle disagreements between unions and management not only without interruption of production, but also in accord with policies conceived in the interest of the nation as a whole.

Not all labor leaders, any more than all corporation executives, recognize this new order, or are capable of exercising creatively the responsibilities to the community which rest upon their shoulders. There is corruption on both sides—though fortunately this occurs only in a minority of organizations. More frequently there is shortsighted inability to recognize the needs of the whole community while seeking immediate gains. Sometimes strikes occur which greatly inconvenience the consuming public, including industries and workers not immediately involved in the dispute. Unfortunately, strikes make the headlines, whereas peaceful settlements are not often regarded as news. There are many unions which have bargained collectively with employers for decades without incurring any serious interruptions of production because of inability to reach agreement. Statistics of the Department of Labor show that man-hours per year lost by strikes and lockouts have seldom constituted more than 1 per cent of the man-hours of work contributed by the labor force as a whole.

Most labor leaders, like most industrial managers, have learned by experience, if not by formal education, that their power to benefit those whom they represent is largely dependent on the health and growth of the nation's economy. There are occasions, in both cases, when the immediate interests of the organization seem to run counter to the public welfare. In the case of labor, this type of conflict often arises when workers are displaced by new methods or equipment. Nevertheless, intelligent leaders know that increased productivity in the long run cannot be halted and is indeed the main source of economic benefit to all, including wage-earners. Such conflicts in many cases have been resolved by plans which allow the technical improvements but provide for the displaced workers, while employees who are retained share the general gain in higher wages and shorter hours. As we shall see in Chapter 10, the number employed in the long run has grown more in industries in which productivity has advanced rapidly than in those which have made less gain in efficiency.

The shift from a free labor market to modern collective bargaining, coupled with the shift from something like a free, competitive market for goods to administered prices and professional management of business, makes national economic planning possible in a democratic nation, just as it makes national economic planning essential. The expectation that those two powerful groups—labor leaders and corporation managers—will voluntarily cooperate in achieving economic goals outlined in the interest of all may not be wishful thinking. Together they are in a position to exert powerful influence on what is probably the most backward and inefficient institution in American society—the Congress of the United States.

There is an ancient but persistent belief held by some politicians that business has an interest in keeping the national government as far as possible from "interfering" with economic affairs, which are supposed to be the exclusive domain of "free, competitive, private enterprise." These gentlemen may stir up an influential following, but it is difficult to believe that the following will include many business managers of the modern school. After all, successful executives of large enterprises, most of whom have been well educated both by institutions of learning and by experience, are not likely to believe in fairy tales.

NINE

THE RECORD OF STABILIZATION

How successful in diminishing the swings of the business cycle has the United States been since 1945? Two types of instruments are usually identified in analyzing this experience—those called "built-in stabilizers," since they operate automatically without new legislation, and other policies that may be temporarily adopted by governmental or private agencies to counteract recession or prevent inflation.

Built-in Stabilizers—and Others

The built-in stabilizers include taxes on personal income and business profits, and the social-security legislation first adopted in the 1930s.

Clearly, any tax on income is certain to take more money from the citizens when incomes are large than when they decline, while governmental expenditures are not likely to be smaller in slumps than in prosperity. The outcome is that in recessions government pays out more to the people than it takes from them and thus dampens the effect of the downswing. If government has a budgetary deficit even in good times, there will be a larger deficit when taxable incomes diminish, and this will cushion the effect of the recession. This effect is strengthened when the income-tax rates are "progressive," as in the United States, since such a tax takes a bigger percentage bite from large incomes than from smaller ones; incomes rise to higher tax brackets during prosperity, and fall to lower brackets in depression.

The social-security laws adopted in the 1930s were intended to relieve the plight of the unemployed and provide some income for the retired. They also, however, exert a counter-cyclical influence. When unemployment increases, more insurance benefits are paid out, while the tax receipts from employers which finance the insurance diminish as workers are laid off or go on part time. The opposite effect follows from return of the unemployed to their jobs. The retired men and women who receive monthly pensions from the O.A.S.I. do not suffer cyclical variations of that income, but contributions to the insurance fund, regularly collected from employers and employees, do vary with changes in employment and earnings. Charitable assistance to the needy financed by governments—national, state, and local—is of course larger in bad times than in good.

These built-in stabilizers are not sufficient to counterbalance fully the cyclical variations of private income, but they do dampen the swings of the cycle.

Stabilizing measures which may be adopted from time to time but are not automatic include a variety of actions. When a recession begins, tax rates may be reduced—if Congress permits the reduction! Public construction already authorized may be speeded up when private construction is retarded. Credit agencies of the government such as that which underwrites mortgage loans for housing can intensify their activities in recession and curb them when inflation threatens. The Federal Reserve System may provide more credit, or less, according to the stage of the cycle. And private business corporations may plan long-term stabilization of their new investment in plants and equipment, and may control their investment in materials, goods in process, and finished goods—that is, in inventories—which will run counter to the swings of the general cycle, or at least will not augment them.

Structural Changes

The development and use of such measures, plus structural changes in the national economy which have played a major role in cyclical stability, were described by Arthur F. Burns in his presidential address to the Seventy-second Annual Meetting of the American Economic Association in December 1959—"Progress Toward Economic Stability." Dr. Burns was the chief collaborator with Wesley Clair Mitchell in the pioneering studies of the business cycle made for the National Bureau of Economic Research; he served as Chairman of the President's Council of Economic Advisers from 1953 to 1956 and is now President of the National Bureau.

"More than twenty-five years," said Dr. Burns, "have elapsed since we last experienced a financial panic or a deep depression. . . . Over twenty years have elapsed since we last had a severe business recession. Between the end of the Second World War and the present, we have experienced four recessions, but each was a relatively mild setback. Since 1937 we have had five recessions, the longest of which lasted only thirteen months. There is no parallel for such a sequence of mild—or such a sequence of brief—contractions, at least during the past hundred years in our own country." Dr. Burns regards this change "partly as a result of deliberate economic policies, partly as a result of unplanned developments."

First, personal incomes have become more stable because a much larger part of production is carried on by corporations rather than by farmers and small business proprietors. "Fifty years ago the total income of proprietors was perhaps two and a half times as large as the combined sum of corporate profits and the compensation of corporate officers. By 1957 this corporate aggregate exceeded by a fourth the income of all proprietors and by two-thirds the income of proprietors outside of farming." Incomes of corporations do vary widely between good times and bad, but large corporations "will rarely distribute profits at the same rate they are being earned." They try to maintain stable dividends and accumulate retained profits in good times. They therefore act as a buffer between variations in profits and individual incomes. This tendency has been reinforced by the increased use of retained profits for new investment, a practice stimulated by tax policy.

Meanwhile the growth of government and of its expenditures has reinforced the stabilizing effect of taxes. "Fifty years ago [that is, in 1909, shortly before the adoption of federal income taxes] the combined expenditure of federal, state, and local governments was about 7 per cent of the dollar volume of the nation's total output. Governmental expenditures rose to 10 per cent of total output in 1929 and to 26 per cent in 1957. . . . By 1957 the income tax accounted for nearly 70 per cent of federal revenue, and a little over half of the combined revenue of our various governmental units." It might be added that the growth in that part of the labor force which now works for government has directly increased the stability of personal incomes, since government employees are not laid off during recessions.

The built-in effect of unemployment insurance has been

strengthened by the growth in the percentage of insured workers, of which there were none in 1935. Now more than 80 per cent of those who earn wages and salaries are covered—though the benefits are often inadequate. But some benefits are supplemented from private sources. Meanwhile, the ranks of those who receive old-age pensions have increased as the social-security system has matured. "In 1940 only 7 per cent of people of age 65 and over were eligible for benefits, in contrast to 23 per cent in 1948 and 69 per cent in 1958." And there is a growing tendency to supplement O.A.S.I. pensions with private pension plans.

The effect of all these influences on cyclical changes in personal income seems almost too good to be true. In the recession of 1957-1958, although the dollar value of total output of goods and services fell 43 per cent, the total of all personal incomes—after paying taxes—"declined less than 1 per cent, and the decline was over before the recession ended." In the recession of 1953-1954, total personal income after taxes actually increased, but this outcome depended partly on a "tax reduction that became effective soon after the onset of recession."

The effort to diminish cyclical unemployment is not so successful as the gains in sustaining incomes. Between the middle of the nineteenth century and 1919, structural changes in the economy, as technology developed, increased the incidence of unemployment. In the nineteenth century there were many more individual proprietors and relatively fewer employees. In such an economy depressions may sharply reduce incomes but may not cause so much unemployment, since owners of business do not discharge themselves. But the burgeoning Industrial Revolution introduced changes in technology which favored the growth of large-scale manufacturing, mining, construction, and freight-transportation—industries in which "both production and jobs have been notoriously unstable." The absolute number and the proportion of all employees who worked in these industries increased steadily until 1919.

But since 1919 technology and other influences have so increased the output per unit of labor in the goods-producing and transport industries that they do not need to employ so large a proportion of the nation's workers as before. There has been a corresponding growth in those industries which produce not goods but services, and these industries are less influenced by the business cycle—partly because the demand for their output is steadier, and partly because most of them cannot maintain inventories of goods and materials which may become unsalable in a recession. A barbershop does not lay aside a stock of haircuts while waiting for customers to come in and buy them. A telephone company does not store away long-distance telephone calls when subscribers fail to make such calls.

The tendency toward stabilization of employment has also been aided by the relative growth of "white-collar" occupations—which as a rule carry with them salaries rather than wages, and greater security of employment than production workers enjoy. "The white-collar group, which constituted only 28 per cent of the labor force outside of agriculture in 1900, rose to 38 per cent in 1940 and 44 per cent in 1957."

All these influences, however, have not wiped out cyclical unemployment. "In the postwar period, as over the longer past, the number of men and women at work, and even more the aggregate of hours worked by them, has continued to move in fairly close sympathy with the fluctuations of production." What has changed dramatically is the effect of the cycle on incomes, largely though not wholly because of unemployment insurance and old-age pensions. "The size of the income-receiving population has grown steadily and escaped cyclical fluctuation entirely." Note that this statement refers to the number of persons receiving incomes, not to the total of the incomes they received.

Consumer Spending and Cycles

In cycles experienced before World War II, recessions were often aggravated by a reduction of consumer spending which followed the spread of unemployment or part time, due in turn to the effects of the downswing on business investment. According to the account of Dr. Burns in his presidential address to the Economic Association, the course of events was as follows:

Business firms had been expanding their investment in plant, equipment, and inventories during the upswing of the cycle. "Sometimes the expansion of investment culminated because the firms of one or more key industries, finding that their markets were growing less rapidly than they anticipated, made an effort to bring their productive capacity or inventories into better adjustment with sales"—that is, to diminish their investment in new plant, machines, materials, and goods awaiting sale. "Sometimes the expansion culminated because the belief grew that construction and financing costs had been pushed to unduly high levels." Whatever the reason, the diminished purchases of some business firms reduced the sales of other firms who had previously supplied materials, equipment, or buildings. So the recession spread, while "more and more workers lost their jobs or their overtime pay, financial embarrassments and business failures became more frequent, and uncertainty about the business outlook spread to parts of the economy in which sales and profits were still flourishing."

Consumers would begin to restrict their purchases, some through caution, some by necessity because their incomes had diminished or disappeared. Decline in aggregate consumer expenditures decreased the sales of consumer goods by producers, who in turn reduced their expenditures. A downward spiral of spending and incomes was the consequence, as the course of events repeated itself. Recession would thus continue until business concerns cut costs and increased efficiency enough to make more production profitable, consumers began to protect their minimum living standards by spending savings or refraining from new saving, costs of building and of interest on borrowing declined to a point where new investment by business became more attractive, and failures declined.

Recovery, when it came, started with an upward turn in investment, while consumer spending was at its lowest level. Decisions by consumers did not trigger either recession or recovery.

Since 1945—when World War II ended—consumers' behavior has played a large role in moderating recession and stimulating recovery, thus departing from the traditional pattern. They have, the statistics show, "maintained their spending at a high level even after business activity had been declining for some months, so that the tendency of recessions to cumulate was severely checked." And "consumer spending turned upward before production or employment resumed its expansion. . . . Consumer spending has emerged as one of the active factors in arresting recession and hastening recovery." Numerous forces—social as well as economic—may have combined in producing this dramatic change, but it surely is not unreasonable to infer that the protection of consumer incomes by unemployment insurance, old-age pensions, and governmental counter-cyclical fiscal policy in general, has exerted an important influence on the propensity of consumers to keep on buying during cyclical recessions. To these changes, of course, must be added the rapid growth in numbers of white-collar, salaried employees and of the service industries which are not much affected by recessions.

Change in Political Climate

Dr. Burns emphasizes also the change in political climate (briefly described in Chapter 7 of this book) which has modified the anticipations of businessmen and those engaged in finance. "In investing circles, as elsewhere, the general expectation of the postwar period has been that government would move with some vigor to check any recession that developed, that its actions would by and large contribute to this objective, and that they would do so in a manner that is broadly consistent with our national traditions." Managers in the private-enterprise sector of the economy have accepted government intervention as salutary and have, in general, cooperated with the effort because the enterprises with which they are affiliated stand to gain by a stabilized and growing economy. They, like others, sometimes disagree with specific proposals; economists connected with large business concerns, banks, and labor organizations read carefully the President's economic reports and hold conferences to discuss recommended measures. The policy favored by the executive branch of the government is thus subject to the democratic process and contributes to the economic education of all concerned.

The important advance achieved by the inauguration of the Federal Reserve System before 1914 helped to avert money panics like those of 1873, 1893, and 1907. Nevertheless, it did not prevent the banking crisis of 1933. Dr. Burns believes that the subsequent strengthening of the banking system and of financial markets achieved by legislation in the 1930s has played an important role in stabilization—such measures as "insurance of mortgages, the creation of a secondary market for mortgages, the insurance of savings and loan accounts, and—most important of all—the insurance of bank deposits." No longer does fear play a leading role in the monetary sector of the economy; bank closings and failures have become few and far between. Just as important has been the development of counter-cyclical credit policies (described in Chapter 6 of this book) through open-market operations which make credit more available when it is needed to curb an incipient recession. "There can be little doubt that the rather prompt easing of credit conditions, which occurred during recent setbacks of production, was of some significance in keeping their duration so short."

Business Recognizes the Business Cycle

Business management has begun to be educated by the advance of economic science, especially in the area of the business cycle and the national effort to achieve stability. Some business executives have adopted "long-range capital budgets, closer control of inventories, and more energetic selling or some relaxation of credit standards in times of recession." Apparently such measures have not yet been widely enough adopted to exert much influence on cyclical changes in investment of fixed capital, which, according to Dr. Burns, "has remained a highly volatile activity." (Fixed capital consists of buildings and equipment, as distinguished from materials, goods in process, and finished goods awaiting sale.) However, "businessmen of our generation manage inventories better than did their predecessors. The inventory-sales ratio of manufacturing firms has lately averaged about a fourth less than during the 1920s, despite the increased importance of the durable-goods sector, where inventories are especially heavy. The trend of inventory-sales ratio has also moved down substantially in the case of distributive firms." The consequence is a tendency "to reduce the fluctuations of inventory investment relative to the scale of business operations, and this in turn has helped to moderate the cyclical swings in production."

Dr. Burns concludes that the more important of the tendencies that have favored cyclical stability are likely to continue. Nevertheless, he carefully avoids complacency—as, indeed any thoughtful person who lived through the complacency of the 1920s and the subsequent debacle must. Disaster often strikes at the very moment when people expect nothing but a continuance of good fortune. "A lesson of history, which keeps resounding through the ages, is that the most reasonable of expectations sometimes lead nations astray." It is wise to be aware of the possibility of developments which might be less fortunate. "In view of the inherent variability of business cycles and our still somewhat haphazard ways of dealing with them, there can be no assurance that episodic factors will not make a future recession both longer and deeper than any we experienced in the postwar period."

Unfinished Business

One of the possible dangers is "secular stagnation"—that is, a retardation of the long-term economic growth which in the past has raised levels of living of the population. Some economists mistakenly called attention to this danger in the late 1930s; though they were wrong then, "their warning helped to avert the danger of chronic unemployment." This danger might recur. Another peril is "secular inflation"—which has been taking place because in recent recessions prices have fallen little or not at all, and the price increases "that customarily occur during periods of expansion have therefore become cumulative." There are also difficulties in international economic transactions which might cause trouble—aside from the mere loss of gold—because of a recurring deficit in the international balance of payments of the United States. Unless this deficit is brought under control, "our nation's ability to pursue contracyclical policies during a business recession may be seriously hampered."

Although progress in reducing economic instability constitutes "one of the triumphs of this generation . . . our economy will continue to undergo changes, many of which were neither planned nor anticipated." We shall need "resourcefulness and courage in deliberately modifying the structure of our economy so as to strengthen the force of growth and yet restrain instability."

Opportunities to do so, brief mention of which concludes Dr. Burns's address to the economists, include the following:

"Monopoly power, which is still being freely exercised despite all the exhortation of recent years, can be curbed by moving toward price and wage control or, as many economists still hope, by regenerating competition. . . .

"Costly farm surpluses can be further encouraged by government or discontinued. The problems posed by the slums and the inefficient transportation of many of our cities can be neglected or attacked with some zeal. The inadequacy of our unemployment-insurance system can be ignored until the next recession or corrected while there is opportunity for judicious overhauling."

The next following recommendation was one made while Dr. Burns was chairman of President Eisenhower's Economic Council, and repeated by President Kennedy after his inauguration. "In general, our governmental authorities can deal with recessions by trusting to improvisations of public spending, which often will not become effective until economic recovery is under way, or by providing in advance of any recession for fairly prompt and automatic adjustment of income-tax rates to a temporarily lower level of economic activity." This suggestion has not, at this writing, been accepted by Congress. As a deliberative body, Congress is not adapted to prompt action and usually does not facilitate promptness in any other branch of government. Nor is a suggestion for "automatic adjustment" of tax rates welcomed by legislators who, jealous of their Constitutional power to levy taxes, customarily occupy many months, if not a year or two, in considering changing, and passing (or rejecting) proposed tax legislation.

Dr. Burns ended his address with a plea for effective economic planning of national policies—which Congress did endorse in 1946 by passing the Employment Act. "The coordination of governmental policies, which may make the difference between success or failure in promoting our national objective, can be left largely to accidents of personal force and ingenuity or it can be made systematic through an economic policy board under the chairmanship of the President. These and other choices will have to be made by the people of the United States; and economists—far more than any other group—will in the end help to make them."

Though Dr. Burns did not say so, it is obvious that not many economists will favor proposals from the radical right to abolish the chief instruments of stabilization such as progressive income taxes, insurance against unemployment, old-age pensions, and democratic planning of economic policy.

TEN

ECONOMIC GROWTH

Citizens of the United States are known, both by themselves and by other inhabitants of the world, as a people who have felt a close relationship between bigger and better. They expanded their territory across a wide band from the Atlantic Ocean to the Pacific; their population grew rapidly, at first by a high birth rate, later by immigration from many older nations. A rich heritage of natural resources enabled them to multiply their possessions; ingenious inventions and a developing technology led to mass production and big business.

Recently their traditional supremacy in production and distribution of goods and services has been challenged by a new revolutionary nation under Russian Soviet rule, the announced economic goal of which has been to "catch up with and surpass" the United States economy. And, still more recently, the nations of Western Europe, stimulated by American technology and aided by both grants and capital investment from the United States, have joined these Olympian games. Americans, like spectators at a global athletic contest, cheer producers who defend the championship of their country in the growth league of the Big Two, or the Big Six.

In a more sober but perhaps more valid aspect, as we have seen in Chapter 3, persistent growth of real personal income has made possible two tangible scores for the inhabitants of the United States. First, it has greatly alleviated poverty by increasing incomes in the lower brackets—and has done so without diminishing incomes in the higher brackets. This is a relatively painless way of approaching a less unequal distribution of goods and hence a more democratic society. Second, growth of income has made possible a general rise of levels of living which, though it does not yet approach affluence for the majority of citizens, does provide time and opportunity for activities other than the mere battle against hunger, cold, and disease.

The Employment Act of 1946 plainly directs governmental agencies to seek not merely "maximum employment" but "maximum production"—and therefore, of course, to maintain economic growth. Any success in checking the downswings of the business cycle will serve both these objectives. Growth over the long term is aided when the cyclical upswing can start from a relatively shallow trough, just as it is aided when the upswing itself is vigorous. Chapter 9 has already touched on the recent record of the business cycle. What about economic growth regarded as a continuation of the long-term or, as economists frequently call it, the "secular" trend?

The Long-term Record

In a study presented in 1960 to the Congressional Economic Committee, Raymond W. Goldsmith estimated that the real gross national product in the United States—in terms of dollars which could buy as much as in 1929—increased at an average yearly rate of 3½ per cent from 1839 to 1959. Anyone who has observed the effect of compound interest on a savings-bank account knows that, over a long period, the repeated addition of interest, even at a percentage that seems small, will greatly augment the principal. The same process is at work in growth of the gross national product. It has become a standard procedure to measure the economic growth of nations by the yearly rate of increase in real gross national product.

The figure so derived, however, is somewhat ambiguous as a measure of actual improvement in welfare. In it, to be sure, the effect of changes in prices has been roughly neutralized. But what about increase in population? A bigger population would be expected to produce a bigger aggregate product. Indeed, unless the increase of product exceeded the increase in number of people, the individuals concerned would gain little or nothing. Perhaps their nation would become more powerful because of mere size—but even this is dubious. Hordes of people without adequate incomes have not, in the past, exercised great power in international affairs—as is shown by the cases of India and China.

The Goldsmith study therefore also included a calculation of the average yearly gain per head of population (or, as

American economists frequently put it—in bad Latin—"per capita"). This gain over the 120 years since 1839 averaged 1⅝ per cent annually. Such a gain, though perhaps almost unnoticeable by the individual citizen in any one year, accumulates significantly in the long run. A still further refinement records the gain in the personal consumption of the people. Personal consumption has occupied about four-fifths of the total gross national product, the other fifth representing chiefly investment by business and public agencies. In the Goldsmith calculation of growth in consumption, there is also an adjustment to account for changes in composition of the population by age and sex. This brings the average percentage gain to consumers down to 1½ per cent for each person annually—enough to count heavily in the long run.

It would be a serious error to suppose that the average increase in product or income over a long period of years means that precisely the same percentage gain can be found between any one year and the next. Variations frequently occur; the gain is smaller in some years than in others. Even to measure the gain over a few contemporary years is difficult, because the business cycle is always in the course of its ups or downs; to make allowances for these choppy waves requires a longer perspective.

Dr. Goldsmith minimized the effect of short-term variations by using a five-year moving average with which to plot his growth curve. This statistical device may easily be understood by those not familiar with it, if they have ever watched waves breaking on an ocean beach while the tide is rising. If you wished accurately to measure the advance of the tide, you could not do so by measuring the advance of any one wave beyond that of the preceding wave, since waves are not of equal size. You could make a much better estimate if you measured the advances of five waves in succession, divided the sum of these advances by five, and if you then averaged the gain of the latest four of these waves plus that of the next one. Your two averages would be successive members of a statistical series "smoothed" by a moving average of five units.

Having derived his smoothed curve of the average yearly economic growth, Goldsmith plotted its upward trend according to what is called a "ratio scale." This is a device in which the trend line is straight if the average percentage gain is the same between any two equidistant points. It thus indicates a trend of the percentage gain, not the absolute quantities. The actual percentage gain in this chart fell below or exceeded the straight-line trend by more than 10 per cent only on three occasions between 1839 and 1959. It fell more than 10 per cent below the trend during the Civil War and the depression of the 1930s. It rose slightly more than 10 per cent above the trend during World War II.

On the basis of the record, therefore, one might expect a rate of growth that varies from year to year and is modified over short periods by the cycle but is not likely to depart far from its historical percentage trend except in infrequent crises associated with war or a near breakdown of the private-enterprise economy. One more refinement should be mentioned, however. Moses Abramowitz, in his study of the "long swings" of approximately twenty years' duration, measured them as variations in the long-term rate of growth. If a current year on which attention is centered lies on the downward side of the long swing, you might reasonably expect a smaller yearly advance in growth than if it were on the upward side. The latest upswing apparently terminated in the mid-1950s.

The real gross national product—at 1962 prices—increased rapidly after the postwar reconversion of 1945-1946. Between 1947 and 1950 it gained about 12.8 per cent, and under the stimulus of the Korean War it jumped about 18 per cent from 1950 to 1953. Thereafter it settled down to a jog-trot, with a gain of about 7 per cent from 1953 to 1956, 7 per cent from 1956 to 1959, and about 10 per cent from 1959 to 1962.

Policies to Stimulate Growth

Many economists, both in the government and outside it, sought anxiously in the early 1960s for ways to accelerate the rate of production. A chapter of the 1962 Economic Report of the President was devoted to the subject, and the report of 1963 returned to it. The Committee for Economic Development, an organization of prominent businessmen and bankers, issued in December 1962 a special report, *Reducing Tax Rates for Production and Growth.* A chart in that study showed graphically where the trouble seemed to lie. Entitled "Per Cent Change in Final Demands for Real G. N. P., 1957-1962," it portrayed the percentage increase of the main classifications of purchases within the total, which during that period had risen about 15.1 per cent. Growth of consumer purchases was 16.5 per cent. Nonfarm housing had grown by the ample percentage of 27.5 per cent; state and local government spending almost as much—26.4 per cent.

Federal government purchases had increased by a slightly smaller percentage than the total gross national product—13 per cent. But standing out like a black shadow was the record of spending for plant and equipment by private business. This had actually shrunk between 1957 and 1962—it had fallen about 1.9 per cent.

"The significance of the decline in private business investment," wrote the authors of the C.E.D. report, "is two-fold. First, it keeps us from employing our labor force and productive facilities at a satisfactory rate. Second, it keeps us from raising as rapidly as we might our capacity to produce efficiently. The first effect could be offset by a further increase in other expenditures. But the second effect cannot be offset in this way. There is no good substitute for a high rate of investment as a means of getting a high rate of economic growth in a free society.... From the possible means of getting to high employment and high production today we should choose the means that contributes most to growth in output per worker." The amount of money spent for investment in plant and equipment—in "constant dollars"—had reached its high point in 1956. As a per cent of the gross national product its peak had occurred in 1957.

The governmental action generally recommended to encourage investment in plant and machinery consisted of tax incentives. In 1962 the corporate income tax was revised to give business some tax credit for profits reinvested by the company, and a change was made in the rules for depreciation of machinery and equipment which would make it cheaper to replace obsolescent equipment with more highly productive devices. In January 1963 the Council of Economic Advisers recommended, and President Kennedy proposed, a general revision of taxes which, among other changes, would reduce tax rates on corporate profits and on personal incomes, in order to stimulate investment.

Productivity

A mere enlargement of plant and equipment used for production will, of course, tend to enlarge output, provided the labor required to operate the additional plants is available. The spread of mechanical, power-driven industry in the United States is in large measure responsible for the growth of the national product. At any one time, however, the labor force is limited, and not even the most advanced nation can produce more than the available supply of sufficiently skilled and competent operatives, with good management, can turn out.

But one development has long been at work to increase the output of the nation more rapidly than would have been the case if growth depended solely on the number of available workers. The output has grown faster than the input of labor. It has done so because the *productivity* of the essential factors has increased. Investment in education and training has enlarged the contribution of the employees per hour of work. Investments in technology have bought more efficient machinery and other equipment, the evolution of which has never, so far, come to a halt. Each man-hour therefore can, with new equipment, produce much more as time goes on. Also, the science and art of management has made great strides, especially since World War I.

Solomon Fabricant, Director of Research of the National Bureau of Economic Research, in the fall of 1962 contributed three articles on productivity to *Challenge*, a monthly periodical devoted to economic affairs. Dr. Fabricant's data were derived from several studies made by the National Bureau—especially one on productivity by John W. Kendrick—though the bureau is not officially responsible for Dr. Fabricant's articles.

The first and most comprehensive measure of productivity is the familiar "output per man-hour," which is the ratio between total output and the total hours of the operatives. Change in this ratio "reflects the combined effect of changes in *three* things": (1) those in "efficiency," which "result from changes in technology, economic organization, management skills," and some other factors, (2) those in "labor quality per man-hour," (3) those in "tangible capital per man-hour." Thus it reflects changes in the knowledge and skills of engineers and managers, changes in the quality or aptitude of labor, and changes in the machinery or other equipment provided by the employer. All three may advance, or one or two may advance. "Output per man-hour will reflect the net balance among the three changes possible (each given its proper weight)."

Between 1889 and 1960 productivity in the United States, measured in this way, grew at an average annual rate of 2.4 per cent in the private sector of the economy. If the government sector is also included, the annual rate of growth was 2.2 per cent for the whole economy, but the figures for government are "rather rough and uncertain."

Dr. Fabricant comments: "A figure of 2.2 to 2.4 may seem small, but it is not. Such an annual rate means an increase of about 25 per cent in a decade, and a doubling in thirty years. Few countries have long-term records that look as good as this. Indeed, many countries would be very happy to have their *current* level of output equal to what we *add* in an average decade. Over the larger part of the globe output per man-hour is less than 25 per cent of the U.S. level."

These rates of growth constitute an average of figures which fluctuate from year to year, and from prosperity to depression. A major change, however, has occurred since 1919—in other words, since World War I. Before that date the average annual rise in output per man-hour was 2 per cent; after it, the average annual rate became 2.6 per cent. And in the fifteen-year period after the end of World War II—1945 to 1960—the average rate of increase was more than 3 per cent a year.

Productivity and Wages

What is the relationship between the increase of productivity and wages? The question of what *ought to be* this relationship is frequently raised in collective bargaining. Unions may demand, first, a change in money wages which will match the upward trend of the "cost of living," and, second, an upward adjustment of the "real wages" so calculated, by a percentage which represents the gains in productivity which have occurred. Sometimes they ask a percentage rise in real wages parallel to the gain in productivity of the establishment in which they work; sometimes they ask a rise parallel to the nationwide gain in productivity.

Dr. Fabricant in his articles on productivity does not attempt to decide whether wage adjustments linked to productivity are fair, or desirable for the general health of the economy. He does, however, provide valuable information on the basis of which others may be better equipped to make such judgments. Specifically, he examines the record of what *has* happened.

His first contribution to this problem compares the course of real wage earnings per hour in the private sector of the economy with the course of output per man-hour in that sector. Real wages are, of course, the money rates modified to account for changes in prices paid by consumers. Wage earnings in this calculation include all the "fringe benefits" which employers pay, such as contributions to pensions and other welfare funds, both public and private. The findings show the following important facts:

1. "Real hourly earnings rose," between 1889 and 1959, "at an average rate of 2.4 per cent a year. This is equivalent to a rise of 27 per cent per decade, or to a doubling in just under thirty years—a very substantial gain."
2. "The rate of increase in real hourly earnings was much the same as the rate of increase in output per man-hour"—for the private economy as a whole.

These statements cover the long-term trend; there was variation in the gain of real hourly earnings and output per man-hour from year to year. It is important also to note that they cover the average gains in real earnings for the whole private economy, and also the average gains in productivity for that economy. Some industries, and undoubtedly some firms within each industry, made more rapid gains in productivity than did others.

The next calculation by Dr. Fabricant answers the question whether the gains in real hourly earnings in each industry parallel more closely the gains in output per man-hour by that industry or the average gains in output per man-hour for the private economy as a whole. This answer is important, because some industries have registered much greater gains in output per man-hour than others. The figures for 1899-1953 cover twenty industries, ranging from electric utilities, which made a very large gain in output per man-hour, to anthracite coal mining, which gained very little. The figures show that the percentage increases in real hourly earnings of labor in each of the twenty industries were much closer to the average gain in output per man-hour for the private economy as a whole than to the output per man-hour of the specific industry. For example, in electric utilities, the gain in real hourly earnings from 1899 to 1953 was about 200 per cent and the gain in output per man-hour was more than 2000 per cent, whereas in anthracite mining the gain in real hourly earnings was slightly more than 250 per cent and the gain in output per man-hour was less than 150 per cent.

Productivity and Prices

Anyone who reflects on these comparisons is likely to jump

to the conclusion that the industries which made the greatest gains in productivity, and did not grant any larger wage boosts than industries which made small gains, must be exploiting labor or the consuming public or both. But that conclusion would overlook two important questions—first, what about the expenditures on plant and machinery that were essential to productivity gains, and second, what happened to the prices charged to consumers by the various industries?

Dr. Fabricant presents an illuminating picture of this situation also. If one arranges the industries in descending order of change in output per unit of *labor and tangible capital,* and then records the price changes made by each of these industries between 1899 and 1953, one finds that, by and large, the industries which have made the largest gains in productivity have also made the largest reductions in their selling prices, whereas those with little or no gains in productivity have increased their prices. For example, electric utilities made a gain of nearly 600 per cent in output per unit of labor and capital and *decreased* prices by more than 80 per cent. Lumber products, on the other hand, suffered a loss of more than 30 per cent in productivity and *increased* prices about 200 per cent.

These trends cover a long period—more than fifty years—and include a good deal of variation from year to year and decade to decade. Yet, according to Dr. Fabricant, "Given time for necessary adjustments, competition makes for equality of price and cost per unit. . . . And efficiency—output per unit of labor and capital—is a major determinant of cost per unit." Incidentally, the reader should remember that an industry which reduces prices as its unit cost of production declines can often make larger profits than if it had failed to reduce them.

Such figures do not lay the basis for a formula by which real wages should be raised, or prices reduced, in any one year. Many complications are involved. "During short periods . . . less time is available for adjustments between prices and costs as conditions alter." In industries which are not fully competitive "there are obstacles to the adjustment of prices to productivity. But these obstacles will usually be overcome in time, for, in the long run, there is more competition than is commonly supposed." Among other influences, "the immediate impact of increased demand, for example, is largely on price and product. Until new plans are constructed by companies already in the industry or by outsiders attracted by the high profits, prices will be out of line with costs and with productivity. Decrease in demand, perhaps because foreign competition has become intensified, will work in the other direction: the immediate impact may be a fall in relative prices and profits, with prices remaining out of line with costs and productivity until capacity has been retired."

"All the available statistics are rough, and for many industries quantitative information is lacking." We do not know much about productivity in the service industries, in which units of output are not so simply counted as in industries which deal in material goods. Statistics for the government sector of the economy—which produces mainly services—do not tell us much about productivity. And appropriate modifications for changes in quality of the product are difficult to make. The National Bureau of Economic Research is now attempting to obtain better information in these fields—which are of increasing importance since service industries are growing faster than those engaged in material production.

What about the effect of increasing productivity on employment? Wage-earners have worried about this ever since the beginning of the Industrial Revolution in Great Britain in the early nineteenth century, when hand spinners and weavers were being superseded by power-driven machinery. Now the magic wand is "automation." Dr. Fabricant has something to contribute to the answer to this question also.

The "direct effect of increases in productivity (which for this purpose is best measured by output per man-hour) is to reduce employment. . . . But there are indirect effects, and these may not be ignored." Increase in productivity in a given industry often leads to a reduction in the selling prices charged by the industry. "If the response of demand to the decline in price is large, the resulting rise in output will exceed the rise in output per man-hour, and the number of man-hours worked in the industry will go up, not down. . . . In the long run, industries in which productivity has risen more rapidly than in the economy as a whole have (more often than not) raised their employment by a *larger* percentage than did industry generally, and not by a smaller percentage, as might be supposed. And we find, correspondingly, that industries in which productivity has lagged have (more often than not) raised their employment *less* than industry generally—or have actually cut employment."

Though these reassurances are comforting, one must not

overlook the qualifications. The situation favorable to more employment develops "in the long run," and there are exceptions implied by the "not" in the phrase "more often than not." In the short run, rapid technological improvements may throw men and women out of work. And industries which are declining because need for their output has not much increased may employ fewer wage-earners even though they have a long record of improved productivity. Though Dr. Fabricant has not discussed these exceptions, he would agree that they may present difficult problems. The plights of unemployed former coal miners and railroad men in the early 1960s are cases in point.

Unemployment and Inflation

There is always some unemployment, even in the most properous times. Some industries are seasonal and lay off workers temporarily in the slack seasons. Some workers quit one job, because they do not like it, and look for a better one. Some families move from one location to another, and members of the family who have had jobs now must look for new ones. Some new entrants to the labor force who have been in school or college are looking for their first full-time employment. As a rule of thumb, the statisticians who deal with unemployment figures expect that about 4 per cent of the labor force will be temporarily unemployed even in the best of times. This type of unemployment is usually called "frictional" by economists.

In the early 1960s unemployment rose to between 5 and 7 per cent of the labor force even during the top months of the business cycle. Many of the government officials charged by law with the duty of maintaining "maximum employment" concluded that such a large quota of job seekers indicated that measures must be adopted to stimulate demand in the national economy, so that employers would be compelled to enlarge their working forces in order to satisfy their customers. This reasoning lies behind the provisions of tax legislation, recommended in 1963 by the President, which called for tax reductions, not only for business but for individual consumers, so that "disposable incomes" might increase and consumers might have more to spend.

This legislation was expected, when passed by Congress, not only to reduce unemployment but to stimulate economic growth throughout the economy. One effect of the recommended changes would be a deficit in the cash budget of the federal government, at least temporarily. That would mean that government was pumping money into the economy to enlarge output and employment. The enlargement would increase the national income and consequently the yield of tax receipts, so that a surplus in the federal budget might appear in future years, even if federal expenditures were not reduced or were somewhat increased.

When the government spends more than it collects in taxes, it must, of course, borrow enough money to make up the difference between tax receipts and expenditures. It does this by offering government bonds or short-term securities for sale. If the purchasers of these instruments pay for them out of their savings, no expansion of the total amount of money occurs. But if, as usually happens, many purchasers borrow from banks to buy the new securities—or if banks themselves buy them—then the total amount of money is increased. The banking system may cooperate in this process by making credit "easy." In that case money is pumped into the economy and total demand is enlarged. That is exactly the outcome desired by the government when it wishes to stimulate demand throughout the economy so as to increase incomes and diminish unemployment.

But the increase in demand may lead not only to more production but also to higher prices. Here and there capacity will turn out to be limited, or skilled help scarce, or supplies of materials short, as demand rises. When the goal of "full employment" is still some distance away, less of the increase in demand will be dissipated in the form of higher prices and more will be effective in the form of a greater volume of sales, a higher rate of production, and more employment. The closer the goal is approached, however, the greater will the pressure on prices be. For an economy with 6 per cent total unemployment—that is, 2 per cent nonfrictional unemployment—is an economy that is operating on the average at something like 98 per cent of reasonable capacity. Then some of the money pumped into the economy takes effect, not in more real income, but in rising prices. The country experiences what is ordinarily called "inflation," which benefits chiefly speculators who gamble on making money not by producing anything but by a process of buying cheap and selling dear. Inflation damages the large number of citizens who live on fixed incomes—for example, the recipients of pensions and annuities—and others who cannot increase their incomes as rapidly as prices rise. In the end, if rapid enough, it may lead to a collapse of the speculative markets and perhaps a panic to be followed by sharp depression.

Also important are the adaptability and capacities of the labor force, and particularly of its unemployed members. If the unemployed are ill equipped for the jobs that increasing demand opens up, the new money pumped into the economy will make less of a dent on unemployment than is desired; it will lead to more price rises than many people would consider tolerable. Indeed, the question has been asked whether, under the conditions existing in the 1960s, a considerable part of the 5 to 7 per cent unemployed did not consist of persons ill equipped for the jobs that were open. There is, for example, no longer much demand for unskilled labor, since manual work has largely been supplanted by power-driven machinery. Yet some of the jobless consist of Negroes who, denied equal educational opportunities and coming from regions of abject poverty, are not prepared for jobs that most employers have to offer. The same is true of many teenagers of all races who have halted their education before graduating from, or perhaps even before entering, high school. Another fraction of the unemployed consists of coal miners and railroad men who probably will never find another job in the declining industries where they learned their trades. And may there not be among the jobless looking for work a considerable number displaced by machines or automated processes? It takes a kind of talent to produce, repair, and use these devices different from that possessed by the persons they have displaced.

And, as Arthur F. Burns has suggested, there may be unfilled offers of jobs which those who might fill them never hear of because the federal employment exchanges do not have rapid and efficient facilities to match offers with candidates when the prospective employers and the applicants are not in the same region. There ought to be a system which could compare unfilled offers of jobs with the number unemployed. Only with such a system would we be prepared to define "full employment" or to set a numerical maximum beyond which the percentage of the unemployed would call for measures by the government to increase demand.

The federal authorities on the subject have rightly recognized the need for retraining and for an expansion of public education, especially beyond the primary schools, if the unemployed fraction of the labor force is to be capable of filling the available opportunities. These measures have been recommended by the official planners. But the task of achieving the desired results is difficult and, even if successful, will occupy not months but years. In the meantime, the effort to reduce the number of the unemployed to any fixed percentage by deficit spending intended to enlarge demand may result in some degree of inflation—creeping or leaping. The result will be the same, whether the target is to attain full employment or to stimulate economic growth.

More Economic Science Needed

The economic growth of the United States in the past was achieved without any comprehensive national economic planning of the modern type. The problems involved in deliberate attempts to maintain or accelerate it are therefore largely new ones. As yet, the deliberations on the subject have been based more on theory and speculation than on thorough inductive, scientific research of the kind that has brought substantial agreement among the economic experts on the business cycle or the elements of national income.

An example of the wide differences of opinion on the subject of growth was a symposium sponsored by the American Bankers Association, which was held on February 25, 1963. The economists who spoke and asked questions of one another were recognized authorities. They all made interesting contributions to the subject. Yet Gabriel Hauge, who was appointed to summarize the discussion, was reminded of a remark made to him by a guide on an island in the Caribbean where Christopher Columbus was supposed to have landed in 1494. The guide said, "Christopher Columbus never knew where he was going, he didn't know when he had arrived, and he always thought he had been somewhere else after he got back."

In the confusion of ideas which now surrounds the subject, perhaps one more modest suggestion may be admissible. It is prompted by the findings of Dr. Fabricant briefly summarized in this chapter, which show that the industries which have had the most success in increasing efficiency are those which have most reduced their selling prices over a long period. Apparently, also, they are industries which rank high in their achievement of growth. Suppose the economic planners should attempt to generalize this experience by organizing their ideas about a target for the economy as a whole which would resemble the experience of these industries—a target which would seek maximum growth through gains in productivity, *within the setting of a slowly falling national price level,* but with wages steady or rising, so that *real* wages will move up with the growth in productivity.

Many contemporary economists would regard such an idea as fantastic; indeed, some of them have argued that "creeping inflation" is essential to economic growth. They may be right, but the opposite conclusion might reward careful analysis. Is not a slow but steady fall in prices the most feasible and the fairest way of distributing productive gains among the whole population? Would it not put a premium on efficiency and discourage merely speculative capital gains? Would it not bring together, in private enterprise, the profit incentive and the interest of consumers? Housewives would like it. "Rentiers," who in this country consist largely of people who depend on pensions and insurance, would like it. Colleges and philanthropic foundations, with all those dependent on them, would like it. Taxpayers would like it. It is not incompatible with a steadily rising real income of individuals. And it is, as we shall see in the next chapter, a possible means of avoiding difficulties with our international balance of payments and strengthening our competition in world markets.

There is, furthermore, a historical precedent for a combination of growth and falling prices. The wholesale price index of the Bureau of Labor Statistics (based on 1926 as 100) had a generally decreasing trend between 1866 and 1896. It began with an index number of 116.3 in 1866 and ended with one of 46.5 in 1896. There were, to be sure, fluctuating changes in the intervening years, and there were depressions and money panics—with which we should now be better able to deal. But real incomes had a marked upward trend in the period as a whole. And the index of economic growth cited at the beginning of this chapter did not at any time during these thirty years depart by as much as 10 per cent from the long-term upward trend (3.5 per cent annually).

The institutions, practices, and world setting of those days were of course different from those which now prevail. It is quite possible that a careful historical study would show that what worked then could not work now. Yet even a negative conclusion might throw some needed light on present ideas about growth.

ELEVEN

THE INTERNATIONAL INCOME

There is a habit of thinking which regards nations only as economic competitors. Each nation, according to this idea, should strive to sell as much outside its borders as it can, and to buy as little. The greater the difference between its sales and its purchases, the greater its profit. The first systematic exponents of this view, which flourished in Europe before the American Revolution, were called mercantilists, because they regarded a nation as a competitive merchant.

Economists of every school from Adam Smith on have had no difficulty in demonstrating the absurdity of the mercantile thesis. If every nation were only to sell, who would do the buying? Where is the purchaser who can keep on buying indefinitely without earning anything? Furthermore, what is this "profit" which a nation gains when it exports more goods and services than it imports? Obviously foreigners are getting more real wealth from it than they are yielding in return. They may, for a while, pay in monetary gold, but the gold itself is of no use—except as a formal reserve for money—unless it is to be spent. Gold cannot be spent by the nation receiving it unless at some time that nation buys more abroad than it sells. (Buying or selling, in international accounts, includes purchase or sale, not only of goods and services, but of bonds, mortgages, short-term loans, and direct ownership of business concerns, land, or mineral rights.)

The process of social accounting which is used to reckon the national income may also be applied on an international scale. There is a tendency for the incomes of all nations to rise or fall at the same time, just as there is for the incomes of all the groups within a nation. This is a necessary consequence of the fact that the purchases of any nation constitute the sales of other nations. To have figures for the national incomes of the United States, Great Britain, Canada, France, and other countries, without any figures for the world income, is almost as fragmentary a way of dealing with the subject as it would be to have figures for the state incomes of New York, Pennsylvania, and Ohio, without knowing much about the national income. There are already rough guesses of world income, and some day the figures are likely to be more precise.

One thing we may be sure of. Any world account of foreign trade must show that the sum of expenditures of all nations outside their borders exactly equals the sum of their receipts from outside. For every spender there is a corresponding receiver, just as within a nation. The world cannot buy more than it sells, or sell more than it buys. Some nations may have a deficit in their foreign transactions, others a surplus, but the totals of the two groups balance out. (Accounting of foreign trade is far more complete and accurate than accounting of national incomes in backward nations, and it supports this self-evident truth.)

The figures for the national income of the United States account for a considerable slice of the world income. Approximate estimates indicate that this country, with about one-fifteenth of the population, land area, and natural resources of the globe, turns out more than 40 per cent of the world's industrial production and probably about one-third of all the goods and services of every description. Even by 1929 the national income of the United States was equal to that of twenty-three other countries combined, including Great Britain, Germany, and France. In 1962 imports by the United States constituted about 14 per cent of all the imports of the world. The United States accounted in 1961 for nearly 18 per cent of the world's exports of merchandise.

The consequences of these facts are momentous. The sheer economic bulk of the American republic renders it a strong influence in stability or instability of the world's economy. We could not be greatly injured by any misfortune in, say, Argentina or Sweden, but other nations would necessarily be affected by any important change in our income.

Foreign nations not only require machinery, tractors, wheat, cotton, tobacco, petroleum, and a host of other products from us; they need our orders for what they produce. Ordinarily we do not think of the United States as an importing country. It is not so dependent on imports as most others, yet it has been the largest single importer in the world, next to Great Britain. In the years 1936-1938 our imports were valued at nearly 2.5 billion dollars a year; in 1962 they were worth more than 16 billion dollars.

When employment shrinks in the United States, Americans eat less sugar and bananas, drink less coffee and tea. American industry buys less tin, nickel, chromium, manganese, pulp and paper products, wool, rubber, and dozens of other imported materials. South America and Asia are then thrown into even deeper poverty than usual; Australia, Indonesia, and Africa suffer. In consequence, they buy less from Great Britain and European countries; the manufacturing nations in turn suffer unemployment. In spite of the fact that the bulk of British foreign sales (mainly manufactured products) have not come to the United States, British exports, at least before 1939, followed almost exactly the same course as American industrial production.

The Tangle of Payments

Income equals product on the world scale, just as it does on the national one, yet there are bothersome differences which make the international economy more delicate and intricate. There are no tariff duties or other important controls of trade between, say, Illinois and Pennsylvania. Both states use the same currency. Anyone in Illinois who wants to travel in Pennsylvania, or decides to move there, can do so if he has the necessary means. Neither state restricts immigration from the other. The result is that people in Illinois can buy and sell in Pennsylvania to the extent that cash or credit is available. If one state should prosper less than the other, unemployed workers could look for jobs across the state boundaries. A man who has capital to invest does not worry because state lines may intervene between his investments and his place of residence.

But nations do interpose trade controls at their boundaries. They use different currency units; each important nation has its own monetary and credit management. They require passports and visas; they restrict immigration; they impose customs duties. In consequence, it is often necessary to be concerned with the relative values of currencies, the interrelationship between employment and the exchange rate, and the possible difficulty of paying debts across national boundaries.

Economists have worked out a system of accounting for the international payments of any given country. Such an account is based on the axiom that the payments coming into a country in any given period must equal the payments going out, if changes in indebtedness—called loans or investments (that is, capital movements and purchases or sales of monetary gold)—are included. The same principle could be applied to the external trade of any state or section of the United States, but ordinarily is not, because there is not so much need to pay attention to it, and records of transactions over state boundaries are usually not kept separately from those of transactions within them.

If the reader will look back at the nation's economic budget in Chapter 8, he will see under the heading "International" an item for 4.8 billion dollars of foreign investment for the year 1946. This is the difference between the value of all goods and services received by foreigners during the year from the United States and all those that were received from foreigners by Americans. In other words, it is the year's addition to what foreigners owed us (or were given). The item is a minus one in the budget because we supplied this part of our produce without getting anything currently in return.

A summarized statement of the "Rest of the World" account of the United States for the year 1946 shows how this balance arose. This statement appears in Table 7.

TABLE 7. REST-OF-WORLD ACCOUNT, 1946
(Millions of Dollars)

Net Payments of Factor Income to the United States:		*Net Capital Movement from the United States:*	
Wages and Salaries	8	Long term	3,342
Interest	122	Short term	1,176
Dividends	118	Change in gold stock	623[1]
Branch Profits	198		
Net Purchases from the United States		Errors and Omissions	—118
From Business	4,285	Adjustments for United States Territories	
From Government	1,139	and Possessions	—250
From Persons	—1,097		
Net Current Payments to the United States	4,773	*Net Disinvestment in the United States*	4,773

[1] When the United States *receives* gold, this entry has a plus value, as here.

From the items on the left-hand side of this account it

may be seen that in almost every category, in 1946, foreigners paid more for our services and goods than we did for theirs. (In order to get these "net" figures, outgoing payments are subtracted from incoming ones.) Thus, they paid 8 million dollars more in salaries and wages to Americans than Americans paid to them. On balance, interest, dividends, and branch profits flowed in this direction. Of course foreigners bought huge amounts of goods here, partly from business, partly from government, while we bought much less from them, in part because in 1946 they did not have much for sale. Only the purchases of individual Americans abroad (chiefly members of the armed forces or tourists) exceeded foreigners' purchases from American individuals. The item which includes these purchases is called, in the table, "Net Purchases from Persons." It is preceded by the minus sign to indicate that more purchases were made by Americans from foreigners than by foreigners from Americans. The total surplus of payments to Americans naturally is the value of the excess of exports from the United States over imports to it, including both trade and payments for services, or "invisible exports."

The right-hand side of the table shows how, in general, this excess of exports was financed. Long-term and short-term credits were both used; under these totals is also included the sale here of already existing foreign securities. Naturally the details would show that the capital movement was largely a matter of United States government credits, such as the loan to Great Britain. In addition, foreigners sent over 623 million dollars in gold to help pay for what they needed.

Since not all international transactions can be traced, there is not a perfect balance, and consequently a relatively small item for errors and omissions has to be included. An adjustment also has to be made on account of the fact that while most of the figures cover the continental United States only, some also cover the outlying territories and possessions.

Accounting statements like this are merely records of the truisms about foreign trade which economists have long been reiterating. For example, if the items on the right-hand side of the account had been smaller, foreigners could not have bought so much from us. They either had to borrow the money or pay in gold. Why did they have to borrow? Only because we did not buy from them nearly as much as they bought from us. If the items at the left-hand side of the account had added up to zero, foreigners would not have had to borrow a cent or send us an ounce of gold. Current payments would have been in balance.

The Debris of World War I

In order to understand the world economy and its changes since the Second World War, it is necessary to review briefly some of the more important international developments which followed the victory of the Western European Allies and their associate—the United States—in the First World War, which came to an end in 1919 with Germany's unconditional surrender.

According to the Treaty of Versailles, drafted by representatives of Britain, France, Italy, and the United States, and imposed upon Germany, France annexed Alsace and Lorraine on her northern boundary—the latter a natural part of the coal-and-steel region which adjoined the German Ruhr. In addition, Germany was required to pay indefinitely large sums as reparations for war damages. These burdens were imposed not on the imperial German Reich which had been the aggressor, but on the democratic German republic (the Weimar Republic) which had succeeded it.

The Versailles Treaty and the Treaty of Trianon, which the Austro-Hungarian government was compelled to sign, also separated large regions from both these defeated countries in order to form new, independent nations—Poland, Czechoslovakia, Hungary, Yugoslavia, Albania. This part of the peace settlement was in accord with President Wilson's commitment to "national self-determination." Yet by the European victors it was valued not as a liberal contribution to political freedom but chiefly as a means of breaking up hostile empires. Like Germany, the Austro-Hungarian Empire, whatever its faults, had been a great producer of economic goods, scholarship, and culture; now Austria was left as a relatively small area surrounding Vienna, with only a dubious access to the Adriatic Sea. In essence, the dictated peace terms represented an unstable victory in the centuries-old struggle for European military supremacy. It may be noted that after World War II the newly "self-determined" nations all fell under the domination of Communist Russia.

The economic folly of the Versailles Treaty was promptly and convincingly exposed by John Maynard Keynes—the British economist who subsequently was to develop the general theory now coupled with his name. In his *The Eco-*

nomic Consequences of the Peace the major contention was that Europe—at least Western Europe—was naturally a great market, which before the war had been benefited by its variety of resources and skills and the regional specialization which a large and varied trade area permits. He also noted the importance of the German economy as a highly efficient producer of manufactures. Now Europe had been carved up by new boundaries which would undoubtedly increase customs duties and hamper movements of goods, capital, and persons.

Meanwhile the important German economy, under the regime of the newly established Weimar Republic, was discouraged in attempting to increase its economic output by the provision of the peace treaty that the amount of reparations would grow indefinitely as German national income grew. The necessary sums—in German marks—would have to be collected by high taxes imposed by the central government. Furthermore, marks could not be exchanged for the French francs or other foreign currencies with which the reparations were to be paid unless Germany had a favorable balance of payments in her other foreign transactions. Means of earning foreign currencies were diminished not only by loss of territory in the coal and steel regions of Lorraine but also by the fact that the victors had seized the German merchant marine and colonial dependencies.

Shortage of Dollars and the Gold Standard

For many years before World War I the foreign exchange values of most currencies had remained stable. Although it was not so easy to buy or sell abroad as at home, people were not deterred by any fear that the relative values of pounds, dollars, francs, and the rest were likely to shift widely. The economists had a ready explanation for the stability of exchange rates—an explanation which seemed self-evident to those who dealt in foreign exchange. Suppose a man with pounds sterling wanted to buy something in the United States. Naturally he would need dollars for the purpose. He would buy dollars with his pounds. If the demand for dollars should exceed the supply, the price of dollars (that is, the exchange rate) would rise. This would mean that it would take more pounds to buy in the United States. But the possible rise was limited by the fact that the United States and Great Britain were on the gold standard. Anyone could buy gold with his pounds, and buy dollars with his gold, at rates permanently fixed by the governments. So, instead of directly buying dollars after the rate had risen above a certain point, the British purchaser would buy gold and ship it to the United States. The limits within which the exchange rates could fluctuate were determined by the cost of shipping gold.

During the period between the outbreak of World War I, in August 1914, and the entry of the United States into the conflict, in April 1917, this country was a large and essential source of supplies to the European belligerents. Britain, France, and other European nations paid for their military imports by issuing bonds for sale in the United States—thus protecting their stores of gold and their currencies. As their credit standing began to wane, they also were compelled to sell holdings of American investments owned by their citizens, the income from which had been important before the war in maintaining their balance of payments on a high level. After the entrance of the United States into the conflict, the United States government financed the purchases of the Allies in this country by buying their newly issued war bonds, which now represented debt owed directly to the United States Treasury. The net result was that by the end of the war Western Europe had lost much of its ability to buy from the United States without either going further into debt or increasing its exports to this country. The first alternative was not open to them because the Harding-Coolidge administration demanded repayment of the existing war loans rather than an increase in the debt, and the second alternative was hampered by a sharp increase in United States import duties.

There would have been, soon after 1919, a critical shortage of dollars held by European belligerents and an imminent collapse of the European economy if a temporizing development had not intervened. The United States, becoming prosperous in the 1920s, began to invest huge sums abroad, and particularly in Germany. While this increased foreigners' debts to us and so aggravated the long-term problem, the dollars going abroad temporarily provided foreigners with some of the purchasing power they needed to buy from us. Incidentally, they also provided Germany with foreign exchange needed to pay war reparations. Meanwhile, the high American protective tariff prevented Europe from coming closer to a balance of its current accounts by selling us more goods.

This adjustment worked passably as long as the stream of American foreign investment continued to flow. But the stream began suddenly to drop in 1928. In 1929 and for years thereafter the Great Depression in the United States cut down our orders of foreign goods as well. The resulting scarcity of dollars in European hands deepened world-wide depression and led to many of the governmental obstructions to trade which Americans deplored. Unemployment in Germany helped Hitler in recruiting storm troopers and aided his rise to power.

Except in the case of Hitler Germany, trade obstructions were largely measures of self-defense by foreign nations against the consequences of dollar scarcity. Not having enough gold or dollars, they had to look for other means of buying what they needed; hence in the 1930s barter arrangements, "clearing agreements," and the like were made. Quotas, exchange control, and the other limitations of foreign trade were measures to make sure of getting the most necessary imports. International barter arose when money was lacking, just as barter among individuals sprang up in the United States when, during the depression, money was not available.

World War II reduced British and European foreign investments to an absolute minimum. Lend-Lease, by which the United States shipped to its allies war supplies without demanding either immediate payment or war bonds which would enlarge their foreign debt, retarded this process as far as the United States was concerned, but even here the period of "cash-and-carry" before Lend-Lease went into effect compelled the British and French to sell large quantities of their remaining American securities. In other parts of the world Britain not only sold capital holdings but incurred what amounted to a huge war debt. Even after World War I, in the years 1919 and 1920, Europe still had an income from foreign investment and "invisible" trade items equivalent to about 8 billion dollars today; in 1946 and 1947 this same type of income was a minus quantity—the European deficit was 1.4 billion dollars.

Europe has been in the past, and still is, a great producer of wealth. She imports from the Western Hemisphere only a minor percentage of what she consumes. Yet the imports she needs are vital. Without them her own production would fail. It was therefore necessary to find some way of obtaining all the dollars required. In the short run, the scarcity of dollars to sustain the European population and help build up more production after World War II had to be remedied mainly by the United States.

Two footnotes must be added to this brief summary of the calamitous scarcity of dollars in the rest of the world which existed up to the late 1940s. One is that rising prices in the United States greatly aggravated the difficulty. It is true that the prices of what foreign nations had for sale rose as well, but in many cases these prices did not rise so much. The "terms of trade" for Great Britain usually become adverse in periods of high prices, favorable in periods of low prices.

The other footnote concerns an important aspect of the problem in which little improvement had then been made. Within the United States a locality which does not have enough money to buy what it needs from a more prosperous part of the country, and cannot borrow it, is likely to lose population. People who are hungry and cold migrate to places where better-paying jobs can be found, if there are such places. But migration across national boundaries was so severely restricted that it amounted to a mere trickle. Freedom of trade and absence of currency troubles are consistent only with free movement of people. Western European nations were not eager to solve their problems by losing population. But in nations such as Italy and Greece there seemed no immediate hope for a solution unless surplus population could emigrate, and little future hope unless productivity could be increased and the birth rate fell.

Scarce Goods

Shortage of dollars was, in a sense, a regional problem and, with wise handling and good luck, remained serious for only a few years. Behind it there is a problem as old as the world, though one which has temporarily been obscured here and there by fortunate circumstances. It is the race between population and the means of sustenance.

Strangely enough, through all the misery of destruction during the two wars, population kept right on increasing—in Europe, Asia, and Africa as well as in continents which were never bombed and on which no hostile army set foot. Nowhere in the world was there enough food, clothing, houses, to say nothing of less elementary necessities, to satisfy the need for them. Even in the United States, incomparably richer than other countries and producing much more than in the 1930s, we knew this to be true. Here dollars were far from scarce; the abundance of dollars merely revealed the scarcity of goods. The delusion of depression days—that there were unsalable "surpluses"—was exposed by common experience. The surpluses had been merely goods that people could not buy, not foods that were not wanted.

The scarcity of goods on a world scale was aggravated by special circumstances. In Europe the most serious was the economic collapse of Germany, normally one of the most productive nations in the world. Without the heavy goods and coal formerly turned out by the Ruhr, the Rhineland, and Silesia, the rest of Europe was impoverished. Before World War II the rest of Europe bought more from Germany than it sold to Germans. Germany's surplus industrial production was a powerful help in maintaining Europe's living standards. England in turn had bought more from Europe than it sold there. The triangular circuit of trade within Europe was now broken; at one of its sides was the wide gap left by the disappearance of Germany as a surplus-producer.

Another shortage of goods arose in Eastern Europe (including East Germany). Russian troops had occupied East Germany, Poland, Czechoslovakia, Hungary, Rumania, and other Balkan states; after the war Communists seized power in these regions. From them the Western manufacturing nations used to obtain much of their needed food and raw materials. They no longer could get as much. Aside from political difficulties, and aside from war devastation, the breaking up of great estates and the application of Communist dogma to agriculture reduced the output of grains; even the domestic populations did not have enough.

Finally, disturbances in Asia and other remote parts of the world hampered production and export of goods on which industrial nations depend. Japan, a defeated nation, had to rearrange her war economy to restore her development of modern industry. Neither India nor China ever fed her own population sufficiently, nor was there ever much check to the growth of these populations except famine and disease; war and political change added to the difficulty. Malaya and Indonesia were also in turmoil to achieve their freedom. Would these nations in the coming years produce enough goods for themselves, and would they be able to export increasing quantities?

A restoration of German production, a growth of trade between Eastern and Western Europe, and a period of productive advance in the Far East seemed to be three of the essential conditions for beginning to supply the world's real need for goods. It was even uncertain, according to the Food and Agriculture Organization of the United Nations, whether enough food could be grown for many years to come.

A Peace of Reconciliation

When World War II ended in 1945, the action of the victors belied the old saw that men learn nothing from history except that men learn nothing from history. Their governments—or at least the governments of the United States, France, and Britain—rejected proposals for a punitive peace which not only would impose on Germany war indemnities but would prevent the revival of her industry and reduce the nation to an agricultural region which could not equip a modern army. Hitler and Mussolini had brought ruin to their peoples and had been killed ignominiously—Hitler by his own hand, and Mussolini by enemies among his own countrymen. French, British, and American armies continued their occupation of Western Germany to make certain that any remaining sparks of Nazism would be extinguished; Soviet Russian troops remained in occupation of East Germany and eventually established there a satellite government under Communist control. West Germany became an independent federal republic in 1949—with its capital at Bonn—and the Western armed forces remained only by permission of the new government. Austria and Italy, Germany's wartime allies, also established democratic republics.

The policy of reconciliation with the Germanic peoples favored by the Western powers was reinforced by the potential threat of Stalinist Russian imperialism, which not only imposed Communism on Eastern Germany by a combination of armed force and conspiracy, but took over for the Communist bloc Poland, Czechoslovakia, and Hungary. Western statesmen saw clearly that their great design must be rehabilitation of the economy of West Germany, France, Italy, Britain, and other Western powers.

A similar policy of reconciliation and restoration was adopted by the United States in the case of Japan, on which the first atomic bomb to be used in warfare had been dropped.

The physical war damage in Western Germany required extensive rebuilding; destruction in Japan, though terrible where the two A-bombs had fallen and in Tokyo, was not so widespread. In neither case had the war destroyed the industrious habits and the skills of the population. Other advantages, especially in the case of Germany, were the following:

Limitation of the defeated nation's armed forces released resources of money, men, and materials for civilian production.

Expenditures by the occupying armies for several years added to the income of the government and the people.

New factories, mills, and machinery could take advantage of the latest improvements; much of the obsolete equipment did not need to be depreciated—it was already smashed.

In Germany after the establishment of the Bonn Republic, shrewd economic management on the part of public officials adjusted taxes and government expenditures in such a way as to favor saving and investment in productive facilities and to discourage personal consumption as long as consumer goods were scarce. Although after World War I a combination of too much money and too few goods had brought about a disastrous inflation, a similar calamity was avoided in the late 1940s. The Bonn government also curbed the cartels which had previously existed (and which furnished much of the support for Hitler). Competition was encouraged. The net result was an unexpectedly rapid recovery of West German production under a democratic regime. Although Japan was not so highly developed, her output also recovered rapidly.

Since the indispensable link in the flow of European trade was being supplied by the revival of German industry, other contemplated measures might also have a better chance to rebuild and strengthen the world economy.

Monetary Fund, World Bank, GATT

During World War I foreign purchases in the United States were enormous, and so gold shipments had to be stopped. The exchange rates were arbitrarily fixed by the governments concerned. After that war the world tried to return to the traditional gold standard, but the attempt did not work for long. In the depression of the 1930s exchange troubles multiplied, and World War II gave the final blow to any hope of restoration of the traditional gold standard by Great Britain and many other nations. A substitute was found in the gold-exchange standard, according to which public authorities such as governments or central banks exported or imported gold to settle net international balances of payments and maintain a steady exchange rate.

In planning for the restoration of world trade, which it was hoped would follow the Second World War, one of the first things that had to be done was to make some systematic provision for the stabilization of exchange rates to act as a substitute for the gold standard whenever the balance of payments against any nation threatened too much loss of its gold reserve. The International Monetary Fund was set up for this purpose. Nations which joined it were obliged to contribute capital according to quotas based on their economic importance. The contributions are partly in gold, partly in their own currencies. Exchange rates are fixed by the fund and cannot be altered by any one of the member countries more than 10 per cent without the consent of the fund's directors. In order to maintain the exchange value of its currency, a member nation may borrow from the fund whatever other currency it needs, the limit of its borrowing being set in proportion to its contribution. A great many complicated rules and regulations are part of the Monetary Fund's equipment, but in the main it is a device by which temporary scarcities of any currency in exchange markets are prevented from altering exchange rates. The fund, however, is subject in the end to the same hazards that upset the international gold-exchange standard. If any nation's exchange rates have a persistent tendency to fall, its borrowings from the fund of a scarcer currency may reach its quota; in that event it would be in the same plight as it was under the gold-exchange standard when it had to stop further shipments of gold.

In these circumstances the fund has on occasion permitted alteration of the exchange rate of a nation threatened by too much loss of gold. The change is achieved by a devaluation of the currency unit of the nation concerned, the French franc, for example—that is, legislation which diminishes the weight of monetary gold which it is legally worth. If that change is made, foreign customers are induced to enlarge their purchases from France, since a given amount of, say, dollars or pounds sterling would then buy more French francs than before; this amounts to lowering the prices of French goods and services to foreign customers. At the same time, Frenchmen would be influenced to buy less from abroad, since their francs would now buy fewer dollars or pounds. The result would probably be a shift of the balance of payments in favor of France, which would diminish the gold outflow and might even reverse its direction.

During the 1930s devaluation by a single nation would soon prompt its trading partners to protect themselves, often by devaluation of their own currencies. Competitive devaluation upset world markets and tended to diminish foreign trade as a whole. The Monetary Fund avoids this policy of "beggar my neighbor" by international control of exchange rates, so that an adjustment may be made by a single nation only when the directors of the Monetary Fund agree that the change is in the interest of all concerned. In such cases the fund would not negate its own policy by allowing other nations to engage in competitive devaluation. Incidentally, the difficulty any one nation is likely to encounter in obtaining consent of others to an alteration in the exchange rate of its monetary unit strengthens its domestic impulse to combat price inflation, which, if not duplicated abroad, is likely to discourage its exports and stimulate its imports.

In a larger frame of reference, the International Monetary Fund is an outstanding example of the drift of the modern economic world toward international planning and democratic control, as a substitute for the anarchistic cutthroat competition which had occurred when nations had geared their policies to the classical type of political economy.

The Monetary Fund was created by an international conference held at Bretton Woods, New Hampshire, in 1944—the year before the war ended. The same conference also gave birth to the International Bank for Reconstruction and Development, founded for a different purpose. Nations may borrow from the Monetary Fund for temporary exchange needs, but many parts of the world also wanted long-term loans to repair the ravages of war or to develop their resources. One of the greatest requirements of the peoples was an increase of production, which could be obtained only with new investment in machinery and other capital facilities. The International Bank was designed to encourage such investments on an international scale. Its capital was contributed by member nations in relation to their economic capacity. The bank may lend (or guarantee loans), up to a total limited by its capital, for purposes which its directors regard as productive. This it may do only when private capital is not available for the project in question on reasonable terms. There have been, and are likely to be, important opportunities for development requiring long-term loans at relatively low rates which in the end are self-liquidating but which are properly the task of governmental rather than of private capital.

The International Bank, because of its expert management and its care in the granting of loans, has established a high rating in the world's money markets; its bond issues find a ready sale. The borrowing countries, many of them in a relatively early stage of development, usually prefer to deal with it rather than to accept loans from individual nations, which might insist on requirements that would be open to the charge of influence on the borrowing nation's autonomy or foreign policy. The nation which borrows the money must guarantee redemption, when the term of the loan expires, and regular payment of the interest, in "hard currency"—that is, money which in international markets is "as good as gold." The plans for the projects to which the money is applied must be worked out in detail and must be of a nature which is suitable to the stage of development of the borrower. Such plans are carefully checked by the "World Bank," as it has come to be generally called. The bank also makes sure that the funds are applied only to the project for which they were intended.

The World Bank, with its sources of information and its wide experience, is also equipped to advise underdeveloped nations about their general plans as well as about single new projects. But its original limitations prevented it from financing projects that require "risk capital," such as might directly be undertaken by private investors. Rather, it concentrates on basic public improvements such as governments frequently undertake in developed nations characterized by private enterprise—transport, sanitation, improvement of rivers and harbors, development of mining, power resources.

Private capital for direct investment in business ventures must follow the sort of aid provided by the World Bank, if the basic improvements which it finances are to bear their expected fruit. For this purpose, I. F. C.—International Finance Corporation—was later organized. This agency found it difficult to induce investors from the more highly developed countries to risk their capital in the more backward regions without much the same guarantees about foreign exchange as are required by the World Bank itself, and without other conditions distasteful to the developing countries. Such countries, in addition, frequently wish to plunge headlong into large industrial projects before they have established an adequate foundation.

Eventually the World Bank created a subsidiary to encourage a more risky type of investment—I. D. A. (International Development Association). Like the bank itself, I. D. A. is supported by capital funds from the member governments, but its loans are interest-free or bear a very low rate, and the period for redemption is longer than that required by the bank itself. The contributing governments were ready to accept these terms because it is in their own interest that poverty throughout the world should be alleviated, and they have confidence in the experience and expertness of the World Bank. In 1959 the United States inaugurated a similar agency to stimulate economic expansion in Latin America—the Inter-American Development Bank.

Clearing the Channels for World Trade

A third type of action also has been needed to stimulate trade and production on a world-wide scale. This is the removal of all sorts of trade barriers which were increased during the depression of the 1930s and were necessarily retained or even strengthened for war purposes—tariffs, exchange controls, export and import restrictions, bilateral barter arrangements, and the like. The United States, through the policy of its reciprocal trade agreements, strove with some success to reduce or remove these barriers between 1934 and the outbreak of war in 1939. It had to suspend the effort during the war, but it was successful in obtaining agreements on the part of other nations to abandon obstructions when the emergency would be over. In the fall of 1947 it obtained at Geneva a General Agreement on Tariffs and Trade—usually referred to as GATT—which has embraced the important trading nations outside the Communist bloc and has met periodically ever since its foundation for the purpose of removing or reducing trade barriers by bargaining for mutual concessions.

Fitted out with a means of stabilizing exchange rates for the short run, an institution to encourage world-wide investment so as to increase production and income, and numerous agreements to remove governmental obstructions to international trade, the world, it would seem, could look forward to better times. Yet there was a deep-seated maladjustment which none of these things, and not all three of them together, could greatly modify. Indeed, not one of them could operate as expected until this maladjustment was remedied.

The scarcity of dollars in the hands of Britain and free Europe after the Second World War was the great obstacle. Reconstruction of their productive capacity would require large imports from the United States and other nations in the dollar area. They could not earn enough dollars by selling exports to the dollar area until their capacity for production was enlarged. They could not pay for enough of the needed goods and services by income from, or sales of, their former investments in the dollar area; many of these had been sacrificed to finance two great wars. They could not borrow enough by sales of new securities in the United States, since previous borrowings had not been repaid. The World Bank could help, but its resources were not nearly large enough for the job. In the meantime relief expenditures barely kept alive populations of war-devastated areas. The United Nations Relief and Rehabilitation Administration contributed 1.5 billion dollars in 1946 and 761 million dollars in 1947. The United States gave aid to Greece, Turkey, and Nationalist China, and helped war refugees. Net unilateral payments (gifts by the government) from the United States totaled 2.3 billion dollars in 1946 and 1.8 billion dollars in 1947.

The United States, soon after Lend-Lease transactions during the recent war were ended by its formal termination, agreed to lend a sum to Britain which might help to tide over the crisis. This credit, plus other loans, financed 3.9 billion dollars of the export surplus from the United States in 1947. Liquidation of remaining gold and dollar assets in foreign hands provided, in addition, nearly 4.5 billion dollars. New private investments abroad by Americans in 1947 totaled 756 million dollars. All these sources of money with which to buy from the United States and the rest of the dollar area were not enough to pay for goods the foreign importers needed; the sum of 9.156 billion dollars fell short of the total United States export surplus of 11.5 billion dollars. (The difference was, of course, largely supplied by short term credits.) European nations were scraping the bottom of the barrel; they stood on the edge of bankruptcy. The economy of the United States faced a loss of revenue from exports to its best customers.

The Marshall Plan

To restore the economies of war-devastated nations required a carefully devised general plan to augment their production and trade. A hand-to-mouth policy had been insufficient. Continuation of sporadic loans or grants was not desired either by the recipients or by the United States government. Neither the bankers nor the business borrowers in any of the nations concerned would, in normal times, favor indefinite advances to an enterprise which seemed to have little prospect of earning as much as it had to spend. The bankers and businessmen, however, were familiar with reorganization and financing of temporarily embarrassed enterprises which, by intelligent management, could use borrowed money to become solvent and stand on their own feet. Imaginative leaders on both sides of the Atlantic saw an opportunity to apply similar measures on an international scale. The result was the European Recovery Program, which became known as the Marshall Plan because Secretary of State George C. Marshall—formerly the respected Chief of Staff of the American armed forces—announced it in an address delivered at Harvard in 1948.

The plan offered, to European allies and enemies of the United States in the recent war, as well as to neutrals, grants for carefully planned reconstruction. An American administrator would oversee the whole program. (Later appointed to this responsible position was Paul G. Hoffman, a successful and imaginative business executive.) Engineers and other capable representatives of American industry—including labor leaders—were to be available where they might be of use. A time limit was set at which the aid would cease—1952.

Any nation which accepted the program would be obliged to sanction the plan as a whole. Plans within nations would be subject to the approval of the executives of the program. And—certainly one of the most important provisos—nations which accepted the plan were encouraged to cooperate with one another. Eventually they all appointed representatives to an international Organization for European Economic Cooperation (O. E. E. C.) to clear the channnels of trade among the participant nations in order to make the best use of existing resources regardless of national boundaries. O. E. E. C. brought about reduced import duties, abandonment of import quotas, stabilization of exchange rates, and, where necessary, credits to finance trade deficits for the time being.

The European Recovery Program was accepted by all the European belligerents west of the new Soviet satellite nations. Czechoslovakia, and probably others, wished to accept it but were prevented from doing so by Soviet Russia, which itself rejected the plan. This action was a signal that the "cold war" had begun in earnest. At the moment, the abstention of the Russians insured the very existence of the program, since it made certain a favorable vote in the United States Congress. Many of the legislators would probably have disapproved of any aid to Communists, no matter at what sacrifice.

The grants under the Marshall Plan solved, for the time

being at least, the problems of Western Europe in finding dollars enough to buy abroad what it needed to restore its production. In other parts of the world dollars were supplied by aid from the United States to Greece and Turkey (adopted before the inauguration of the Marshall Plan, when Britain had to cease its aid to strengthen these countries against threatened Russian aggression), by grants to Nationalist China, and by aid to the Philippines, Korea, and the International Refugee Organization. In 1949 President Truman inaugurated a program first known as "Point Four," to offer technical aid to underdeveloped countries throughout the world.

The total of United States government grants abroad, plus the outflow of governmental capital, was 6,415 million dollars in 1947, 5,361 million dollars in 1948, 5,854 million dollars in 1949, and 3,935 million dollars in 1950 (when Britain ceased to need, and rejected, further Marshall Plan help), 3,496 million dollars in 1951, and 2,800 million dollars in 1952, the last year of the Marshall Plan. European recipients had used the aid to increase their output so that they were able to sell more and more exports and could earn enough to buy what they needed abroad. Imports of goods and services by the United States from all sources grew from 8,208 million dollars in 1947 to 15,766 million dollars in 1952. The dollar shortage had disappeared.

After 1950 the United States experienced an annual deficit in its balance of payments, at least through 1962, with the single exception of 1957. This deficit resulted in an outflow of gold and convertible currencies amounting to hundreds of million dollars a year. In addition, foreign purchases of liquid securities in the United States increased holding of these cashable instruments by between one billion and three billion dollars a year.

Obviously the initiative of the United States and Western Europe in restoring war-ravaged economies had registered a stunning success. Nobody was more stunned by it than Americans, who began to worry about a continuing loss of gold by their own country, which only a few years before had held a major share of the world's gold supply. President Kennedy in 1963 welcomed an opportunity to sell to the Soviet Union large amounts of wheat, partly on the ground that the payment would be in gold and would diminish the deficit in the United States balance of payments. His decision was supported by business and agricultural leaders. (The United States government did not directly sell the wheat to the Soviet government but did sell it to private dealers who filled Russian orders in the ordinary commercial world market.)

The irony of this situation was ludicrous. The Soviet leaders, who had haughtily rebuffed American help when it was offered by the Marshall Plan in 1948, fifteen years later dramatized their inability to feed their population because of mismanagement of agriculture in one of the most fertile and extensive grain-growing regions in the world. The United States government (which during that fifteen years had been in the hands of both the major political parties) had encountered so much difficulty in preventing American wheat growers from producing more than American and regular foreign customers could eat that it had been compelled to buy and store huge quantities of grain in order to keep the price within the United States as high as the growers and their political representatives thought fair. Wheat which Americans could not eat was, as far as possible, sold abroad at the lower price determined in the competitive, free-enterprise world market. The Communist leaders who wished to buy our wheat abhorred free enterprise. Of course their people needed the grain. A refusal to sell it would have been inhuman. Also, in permitting the sale, the United States government was lifting a burden from the taxpayers who had furnished the money with which their government had bought and stored the "surplus" wheat, but who were not allowed to buy it at prices as low as those paid by foreign customers.

The Pace of Recovery

Economic growth in Western Europe during the recovery program was more rapid than in the later years; it was also, by and large, more rapid in regions which had suffered the most war damage than in those which had been largely spared. This difference can readily be explained. Suppose, to take an oversimplified illustration, you possess one steel mill, and add one new steel mill of the same size every year. At the end of the first year your productive capacity will have been increased by 100 per cent. During the second year it will have been increased by 50 per cent, since you have added to your two-mill capacity one more mill. During the third year you will have three mills, and to add one more will enlarge your capacity by 33⅓ per cent. And so on.

Obstacles may arise as growth proceeds. The number of

competent workers is not likely to increase so rapidly as the need for their services. The Federal Republic of Germany, for several years after the end of the war, replenished its labor supply with migrants from Communist East Germany. Later the East German government stiffened its border guards and erected the Berlin wall to imprison East Germans who wished to escape. Supplies of necessary materials may diminish and their prices may rise. The installation of technological improvements may approach a limit set by the current state of the industrial arts, so that further growth depends on the pace of invention.

Estimates of the economic growth of the nations concerned differ according to methods of computation. All estimates, however, agree in the ranking of relative growth, as one would expect on the basis of considerations such as those mentioned. The Western European nations have, since 1948, expanded their output of goods and services at a faster rate than that achieved by the United Kingdom, the United States, or Canada. The Federal Republic of Germany led in rate of growth. It was followed, in descending order, by Italy, the Netherlands, France, Luxembourg, and Belgium. The record also indicates a smaller percentage rate of growth in West Europe after 1955 than before. As the United States Council of Economic Advisers states in its Annual Report for 1963, "... the reason has not been a general deficiency of demand; rather it has been pressure on supply. Such convenient sources of growth as technological 'catching up,' the elimination of traditional inefficiencies, and the availability of large inflows of immigrants are beginning to dry up. Unemployment is low and new entrants to the labor force are relatively few."

The European Economic Community

In 1957 Germany, France, Italy, the Netherlands, Belgium, and Luxembourg negotiated in Rome (and later ratified) a treaty which established the European Economic Community, known also as "the Common Market." The Treaty of Rome bound the members to the following objectives:

1. Removal of all obstructions to trade among the members, by gradual steps.
2. A common tariff to be applied to imports from non-member nations.

3. Abolition within the Community of obstacles to free movement of persons, services, and capital.
4. Creation of instruments to serve the principal aims of the Community, such as an investment bank to finance new enterprises, measures to insure competition, a social fund to educate and retrain any workers displaced by changes, and association of dependent overseas territories with the common market.

By another treaty the members established "Euratom" to further the common development of atomic energy as a source of motive power.

The significance of this new development could scarcely be discussed adequately in hundreds of pages. For example, it seemed a possible step toward fulfillment of an old effort to create a unified Europe, such as had not existed since the decline of the Roman Empire. It could be regarded as a cohesion of Western European nations to contain the threat of further inroads by imperialistic Russian power (against which Karl Marx himself had warned). It surely was a long step toward preventing still another armed conflict between Germany and France, such as had led to two disastrous world wars within one generation. Economically, it could be identified as a practical application of the doctrine of Adam Smith, re-emphasized by John Maynard Keynes in 1919, that consumers are best served by an economy of free enterprise in a wide market in which the benefits of specialization and division of labor can best be realized. This doctrine had been well illustrated by growth of the wealth and power of the United States, which occupied from sea to sea a favored part of a continent, and whose constitution provided that there could be no legal internal barriers to commerce or movement of persons.

The power of the United States had just been demonstrated, first by providing indispensable means for turning back Hitler's and Mussolini's armies, and next by applying the economic resources, as well as many of the methods, of restoring Western European economies. The international cooperation among Western Europeans required by the Marshall Plan had already brought about a striking recovery. Should not this cooperation be continued by agreement among Europeans themselves?

A partial but important effort to erase a historical conflict of interest between German and French economic power had just been achieved by the so-called "Schuman Plan," which created the European Steel and Coal Community. The natural basis for a thriving heavy industry lay partly in Germany, partly in France, partly in Belgium or Luxembourg. Some regions had deposits of coking coal; others nearby, but across national boundaries, had iron. Ambition to unify this region politically as well as economically was one of the causes of previous wars. The Coal and Steel Community, now created by treaty, provided an industrial government for the coal, iron, and steel industries in the region as a whole, equipped even with a Court of Justice to make decisions which could not be reached by agreement among possibly conflicting interests. Why not extend the community to all the economic practices of the nations concerned?

By 1963 the nations comprising the European Economic Community had removed 60 per cent of the obstacles to free trade among its six national members. Britain and six other European nations outside the Community had formed a "free trade area" to reduce by steps the barriers to trade among themselves. Now Britain and several other members of the free trade area—Denmark, Ireland, and Norway—applied for admission to the E. E. C. France, under the government of General Charles de Gaulle, prevented their entrance. It began to look as if the effort to broaden the area of trade freedom might be blocked, and the old economic warfare might begin again, although among larger units. Would the common external tariffs of the E. E. C. be so high as to cripple the effort to approach world-wide free markets? Would the Common Market repeat the behavior of former customs unions—for example, the nineteenth-century Zollverein, which abolished trade barriers among separate German principalities, only to result in the formation of the Hohenzollern German Empire, which imposed protective tariffs at its borders? Such an outcome could, for example, protect agriculture in France, Germany, and other members of E. E. C. by import duties which would exclude a large part of the agricultural exports from the United States, Canada, and other members of the British Commonwealth. Would the negotiations made under GATT fail to justify the hope of the United States that, by a series of steps, approximate freedom of world-wide trade would be achieved?

The importance of the European market is indicated by population comparisons. Estimates for 1961 placed the population of the Common Market nations at 170.7 million, of the European free trade area at nearly 90 million, and of the

United States at 183.7 million. The gross output of the E. E. C. was estimated as the equivalent of 173.7 billion dollars, or $1,018 per capita of the population, and of the United States at 475.4 billion dollars, or $2,588 per capita. The E. E. C. exports were valued as almost the same as those of the United States—20.5 billion dollars or 11.8 per cent of the gross national product from the E. E. C., and 20.6 billion dollars or 4.3 per cent of the gross national product from the United States. Imports of E. E. C. were about the same as their exports, or 20.6 billion dollars. Imports of the United States were less, or 16.1 million dollars. All these quantities would be much increased for E. E. C. if Britain and her partners in the free trade area were admitted. Even the income per capita would be somewhat higher.

If enlarging trade areas and abolishing internal barriers to commerce had been good for the material interests of the people within both continents, mutual reduction of import duties and other trade barriers between the United States and Europe should benefit the inhabitants of both continents.

And the Balance of Payments

The international balance of payments of the United States, as noted earlier in this chapter, had for several years preceding 1963 indicated a larger sum of outgoing payments than of incoming ones. The deficit in payments necessarily led either to export of gold or to foreign acquisition of liquid investments in the United States which could be withdrawn at any time. Concern about this continuing deficit did not arise from any immediate peril; the nation still had plenty of gold in its treasury with which to back up bank reserves. Yet the situation might trigger a "crisis of confidence." If speculators throughout the world expected that the United States would be compelled to devalue the dollar—that is, to decrease its gold equivalent—they would hoard gold, betting on the chance that in the future they could buy more dollars per pound of gold. At the same time foreigners who held securities embodying debts payable in dollars would be motivated to sell them, accepting payment in other currencies or in gold. Thus speculators and timid foreign creditors might bring about the very gold shortage in the United States, and the need to devalue the dollar, which they anticipated.

This danger was in part removed by a firm statement by the United States authorities that the dollar would not be devalued. Still desirable, however, was a stimulation of incoming payments, or a reduction of outgoing ones, or both, so that the recurring annual deficit would disappear.

There are numerous classifications of expenditures and receipts across national boundaries, so that a deficit in the total balance cannot be attributed to any one of them alone. Correction of the existing imbalance might be sought in any one or more of these categories. For example, the United States government might reduce its military expenditures abroad, or its grants for economic development, in so far as the proceeds were not spent in the United States. It might discourage new American investment in foreign countries or purchase of existing foreign securities, by taxation of such transactions. Any of these measures might be undesirable on other grounds than immediate protection of the dollar.

There is available, however, a basic policy for the long run which, according both to theory and to recent scholarly assessment of the facts of economic history, should increase foreign payments to the United States in what is by far the largest category of the international account—merchandise trade. *Price and Quantity Trends in the Foreign Trade of the United States,* a study made for the National Bureau of Economic Research by Robert E. Lipsey, and published in 1963, demonstrates convincingly that, over long periods of falling prices of either agricultural or manufactured goods, the total value of exports increased, whereas rising prices tended to check foreign sales. In view of the greatly improved efficiency of industry in Western Europe, reduction of prices of American products, or at least absence of rising prices, would seem to be as desirable for the foreign-trade position of the nation as it would be at home in distributing widely the gains of technological efficiency and in minimizing unemployment. Indeed, this policy might possibly be enforced by foreign competition in those American industries characterized by "oligopoly" and administered prices.

TWELVE

INTIMATIONS OF THE FUTURE

The United States officially recognized the Soviet Union in 1933; Maxim Litvinov came to Washington to negotiate the terms of the agreement. With him he brought a staff of experts to study American industry. It was the privilege of this writer to have a long conversation with a member of the Planning Commission of the Soviet Union; fortunately he spoke perfect English. During the conversation the following dialogue occurred, which I must repeat from memory, since no notes were made at the time. I was the questioner, he the answerer; so that we shall be identified respectively as *Q.* and *A.*

Q. If you were to draw up a five-year plan for the United States, how would you proceed?

A. I don't know; it would be very difficult.

Q. Why would it be more difficult for our country than for yours? [I was expecting him to reply that a capitalist, free-enterprise system is unsuitable for national economic planning. But he surprised me.]

A. Because, in order to plan, one must have a leading objective. For us, it is easy; we must catch up with you. But you already have your great industries, your advanced technology, your railroads, your labor unions. There is nobody for you to catch up with.

Q. But suppose you were compelled to formulate a plan for us, what leading objective do you think you would choose? [Since our economy at the time was limping along near the bottom of the worst depression in history, I expected him to say "full employment" or "economic recovery." But again he surprised me. After a long pause he replied.]

A. I think I would choose the industrialization of Asia and Latin America.

At that time the United States had not embarked on foreign aid; it was many years before the Marshall Plan and before President Truman launched his program for technical assistance to underdeveloped countries. Yet the cogency of the idea, even then, must be clear, either to an adherent of Marxist doctrine or to an economist familiar with the more recent scientific approach to economics.

Marxists (including Lenin) had predicted that mature capitalist economies would come to a standstill because underpaid workers would be unable to buy the output of industries which yielded profits to private owners. This situation would lead to economic imperialism, since capitalist producers in mature economies would have to seek new foreign markets and foreign opportunities for profitable investment.

Economists who did not accept the Marxist doctrine were aware that the low level of production and the disastrous prevalence of unemployment in the United States were traceable to lack of effective demand. The lack of demand, in turn, was largely due to unemployment. Revolving about this dead center, the United States economy lacked business incentive for new investment, which in the end could stimulate employment, wage-payments, and demand. Yet industrial investment might be profitable in underdeveloped regions, and since such development would require exports of machinery and services which the United States could supply it might provide the stimulus desired to start an upward spiral of employment and purchasing power in the United States.

(As it happened later, governmental investment within the United States initiated the revival, and war brought full employment. Postwar aid to development of backward economies was undertaken mainly by governmental agencies, for other reasons.)

When Will the Soviet Union Catch Up?

In 1962 the National Bureau of Economic Research published *The Growth of Industrial Production in the Soviet Union* by G. Warren Nutter. This is one among numerous estimates, but it is one of the most reliable. Dr. Nutter wrote in a memorandum in 1963: "Unfortunately, no research on the Soviet economy can yet be described as definitive, for too much remains deficient and obscure in the basic data. . . . Though results leave much to be desired, one must pause from time to time and summarize what is already known, imperfect as it may be."

Percentage gain in output per year is usually greater when an economy is in an early stage of development—as we had occasion to recognize in the performance of the war-devastated economies after 1945. International comparison of economic growth is likely to be misleading unless countries at the same stage of growth are compared. Dr. Nutter wrote in his book (p. 291): "On the average and roughly speaking, the aggregate level of industrial production was about the same in the United States of 1875 and the Soviet Union of 1913 or 1928. In the United States, production grew at an average rate of 5.1 per cent a year over 1875-1917 . . . ; in the Soviet Union, at 4.1 per cent over 1913-1955 . . . territorial gains excluded."

In concurrent recent years, Soviet percentage gains in industrial production has been faster than those of the United States. Between 1953 (the year in which the abnormal bulge in our output caused by the Korean War had ceased) and 1961, inclusive, industrial production gained in the Soviet Union 75 per cent and in the United States 20 per cent. Does this indicate a startling advantage for Soviet socialism over private-enterprise or mixed economic systems?

Hardly, when official figures of percentage gain of production for the same period exceeded the performance of the Soviet Union in Japan, Pakistan, Venezuela, Brazil, Taiwan, Italy, Greece, West Germany, Portugal, Austria, and Mexico. (These countries are listed in descending order of gain.) The percentage gain of the United States was exceeded not only by these eleven, plus the Soviet Union, but also by twelve other nations. This list, like those above, did not include a country under the dominance of Communism—they were France, India, Finland, Norway, the Netherlands, Sweden, Ireland, Belgium, Canada, the United Kingdom, Argentina, and Chile. Special reasons may be cited for recent growth in specific cases, but in all cases these nations started in 1953 at a lower absolute level than that of the United States.

How soon will the Soviet Union catch up with the United States in total output? That calculation involves several "ifs," as estimated by Dr. Nutter.

If both continue to grow at the same rates as between 1953 and 1961, the Soviet Union will catch up in 1985.

If both continue to grow at the same rates as from 1950 to 1955 (the period influenced by the Korean War), the Soviet Union will catch up in 1993.

If the rate of growth in each nation continues the same as between 1928 (when the first Soviet five-year plan began) and 1955, the Soviet Union will catch up in 2016.

If both grow at the same rates as between 1913 (when the Czar was still in power) and 1955, the Soviet Union will catch up in 2515.

The Soviet Union may never catch up. The United States started with a much larger base than Russia's at the beginning of this international sporting event, so that the annual percentage gain of the Soviet Union may be larger than that of the United States without any narrowing of the absolute difference in the output of the two nations. Dr. Nutter offers a homely illustration of this possibility: "A son will get closer and closer percentage-wise to his father in age but will never catch up, despite the fact that every year his percentage increase in age exceeds his father's." (E.g., son at his eleventh birthday has added 10 per cent of his age at his tenth birthday. Father at his forty-first birthday has added only 2.5 per cent of his age at forty. Father will continue to be thirty years older than his son as long as both live.)

The Warfare State

Ultra-conservatives charge that the United States, as a "welfare state," corrupts rugged individuals, invites governmental bankruptcy by help to its needy citizens, and also lays too heavy a burden on taxpayers by its paternal policies.

Between 1954 and 1961 inclusive (fiscal years ending June 30) the federal government spent in subsidies sums ranging between 4,204 and 7,460 million dollars a year. Of these subsidies, by far the greater part were paid to agriculture and business. Grants for social security, which went largely to unemployment insurance, did not in any year exceed 315 million dollars. Programs for home-owners and tenants brought government a net revenue—incoming payments were greater than outgoing payments. The grants for public housing, urban renewal, and slum clearance, all together, never exceeded 300 million dollars a year. Even if one includes the hand-outs to agriculture and business, total subsidies from the federal government were less than 10 per cent of its expenditures. (These figures are from the official *Statistical Abstract of the United States.*)

The chief welfare measures—old-age insurance and unemployment compensation—are, of course, largely financed by obligatory payments by the insured and their employers, not by income taxes.

About 60 per cent of all federal expenditures in these same years (the lowest percentage being 57.8 in 1959, and the highest 69.4 per cent in 1954) were for "major national security." This item includes military defense, development and control of atomic energy, stockpiling, expansion of defense production, and military assistance to other nations. It does not include civil defense mobilization, space exploration, or flight technology. If taxes are too high and individualism undermined by governmental coddling, the culprit is not welfare but warfare. To be sure, the warfare has recently been largely of the cold variety and may possibly be a preventive of universal holocaust without our giving way before Communist imperialism.

If expenditures for previous wars were to be included, the sums just noted would be augmented by interest on the national debt, largely incurred during former hostilities—which takes about 10 per cent of budgeted federal expenditures—and veterans' services and benefits, which run between 6 and 7 per cent of budgeted expenditures. Therefore, the total current costs of war, past, present, and future, comprise about 77 per cent of federal budgeted expenditures. If all the welfare, plus all expenses of the executive, legislative, and judicial branches of our national government had been wiped out, federal taxpayers could have been relieved of less than one-fourth of their burden in the 1950s and 1960s. If current military expenditures had been canceled, and no desirable civilian expansion of federal spending had been added to the budget, federal taxpayers could have saved at least three-fifths of their contributions to the national government.

Citizens who are closely involved in the warfare state—either as members of the military forces or as executives and employees of the private enterprises which sell their output solely or mainly to the government—sometimes fear unemployment and bankruptcy for munitions industries if the cold war should subside. Other citizens, not directly involved, may remember that the United States did not get rid of the abnormal unemployment of the late 1930s until governmental spending for military purposes rapidly expanded the demand for labor.

Similar fears existed in 1945, when, the war won, the government disbanded armies and canceled war contracts aggregating many billions of dollars. The fears were quickly dispelled by a rapid reconversion of industry to fulfill public demand for goods which had been in short supply. Not unemployment but price inflation soon became the chief peril. Demand, for a short time, exceeded the supply of civilian goods and services. Then came the recurrence of war—in Korea—followed by gradual rebuilding of military establishments as it became clear that plans for universal disarmament would not be accepted by the chief military powers.

The widespread belief that economic distress must necessarily follow disarmament is not supported either by present facts or by experience. The boost to the national economy during the preparation for and the fighting of World War II was, to be sure, caused by huge governmental expenditure. But this expenditure was, to a considerable extent, financed by an expansion of bank credit which accompanied large bond issues by the federal government. In other words, government was truly boosting total demand as it would not have done if the cost of the war had been financed exclusively from taxation. Governmental deficit financing on such a scale would have had the same result on employment if the proceeds had been applied to roads, hydroelectric projects, public building, urban renewal, conservation, education, or any other peacetime project.

The cold-war military establishment, on the contrary, has not been financed to any considerable degree by governmental borrowing, based on expansion of bank credit. About 98 per cent of the cost has been borne by taxpayers. In the twelve years from 1951 to 1962 the federal government borrowed net, in cash, about 23.5 billion dollars and repaid net, in cash, about 18.4 billion dollars. The average yearly excess of borrowing over repayment was about 850 million dollars—between 1 and 2 per cent of the government's annual expenditures. It follows that any reduction of military expenditures would result, in one way or another, in a roughly equal expansion of demand by the private sector of the economy.

If the military establishment were abolished, if taxes were not reduced, and if nonmilitary expenses were not increased, the federal government would have a budget surplus of some 46 billion dollars a year, which might be used to pay off the national debt. In that case the present owners of government bonds would be looking for other good investments, and private enterprise would be flooded by money capital seeking a modest return. But such a governmental fiscal policy is most unlikely.

If federal spending were reduced by the amount of the total military expenditure, the windfall of 46 billion dollars would cover more than is annually paid in personal income taxes, which might be abolished. With the remainder, corporate income taxes could be reduced by one-seventh. The resulting boost to demand in the private sector of the economy would be so gigantic as to stimulate employment of those now engaged in the military establishment—unless the citizens became so surfeited with material wealth that working hours had to be drastically cut in order to find jobs for all.

One other method of utilizing such a windfall remains: the government might use the resources spent formerly on the military establishment for other expenditures in the public interest. There would be more than ample funds to meet every public need—the unfinished business of a humane, democratic order.

No one of these three methods, but rather a combination of the three, would probably be utilized if disarmament should be realized.

Sudden abolition of all military expenditures is not, of course, possible; the calculations applicable to such an extreme course merely serve to dramatize the gains that might result from a gradual shift of resources away from production of the means of destruction. No disarmament at all is likely without reliable agreements among the armed nations.

A report issued in January 1962 by the United States Arms Control and Disarmament Agency, on "The Economic Impact of Disarmament," by Emile Benoit, professor of international business at Columbia University, assumed that annual military spending by this country would rise to 56 billion dollars in 1965, and that thereafter—if international agreement could be reached—it might be reduced by about 38 billion dollars within twelve years, so that in 1977 the nation would be spending for military purposes only 18 billion dollars. If, during this process, the planning agencies of government, employers, and unions did a good job both in taming the business cycle and in guiding the shift from war to peace industries, there would be little danger of depression. It would especially be necessary to find other work for the employees of war industries concentrated in specific areas, such as the Pacific Coast, where booming enterprises are engaged in military aircraft manufacture, shipbuilding, missile and other industries. The talents of scientists and technologists, the author believes, would have much to contribute to nonmilitary production.

In February 1962 the United Nations Economic and Social Council issued a report based on the conclusions of a study group of economists from ten nations, entitled *Economic and Social Consequences of Disarmament*. Among the members of the group were Professor Wassily Leontief of Harvard, noted for his "input-output" analysis, Oscar Lange of Poland, who is well known in the United States, and V. K. Aboltin of the Soviet Academy of Science. The ten agreed that the Communist economies would quickly benefit by the shift of resources from production of armament to output of consumers' goods. Underdeveloped nations might sacrifice income from exports of raw materials used by armament manufacture in more advanced nations, but would gain much by the release of money and manpower from their armies, which would become available to stimulate economic growth. The report concludes that the transition could readily be made with international cooperation, and would be "an unqualified blessing to all mankind."

Investment in Human Beings

Whether a nation is preparing for war or for peace, one essential cannot be ignored—investment in the means of production, without which it would be impossible to enlarge the output of goods and services. Traditionally economists have regarded investment as enlargement or improvement of the physical plants and equipment which are used in production. But now many have recognized that the productivity of a nation depends also on the quality of the persons employed, and that this in turn depends in large part on expenditures, both by the individuals concerned and by the society in which they live, which are required to make possible the health, aptitudes, and skills of those who do the work.

In 1962 a joint committee composed of representatives from leading universities and research agencies, known as the Universities-National Bureau Committee for Economic Research, arranged a conference on the subject; the papers delivered were published in a supplement of the *Journal of Political Economy* of October 1962. Let us glance briefly at some of the findings in a summary—"Reflections on Investment in Man," by Professor Theodore W. Schultz of the University of Chicago. For the sake of brevity in a book addressed to the general reader, his hypothetical conclusions are here paraphrased or condensed.

1. In the United States, production has been rising faster

than investment in plants and equipment. This result must be accounted for by improvement in the quality of persons engaged in production.

2. "Most of the differences in earnings are a consequence of differences in the amounts that have been invested in people. . . . The structure of wages and salaries is primarily determined by investment in schooling, health, on-the-job training, searching for information about job opportunities and by investment in migration."

3. "Changes in the investment in human capital are the basic factors reducing the inequality in the distribution of personal income."

These conclusions are in accord with the findings of research already completed in this field of discovery. Dr. Schultz illustrates the main thesis by a telling comparison:

"Suppose that by some miracle India, or some other low-income country like India, were to acquire as it were overnight a set of natural resources, equipment, and structures including techniques of production, comparable per person to ours—what could they do with them, given the existing skills and knowledge of the people?" . . . Compare this situation with the converse, "a country which would be long on human capital relative to her stock of reproducible non-human capital." In such nations as Japan and West Germany this was the case after World War II; when their physical capital was restored, production zoomed.

A table presented by Dr. Schultz contains figures for the average annual growth of several kinds of contributions to capital in the United States between 1929 and 1957. According to these estimates, investment in persons grew more rapidly than investment in "tangible capital"—buildings, machinery, and other equipment. The annual rates of growth were:

Reproducible tangible capital	2.01 per cent
Educational capital in population	3.57 per cent
Educational capital in labor force	4.09 per cent
On-the-job training of males in labor force	5.36 per cent

Recognition of the importance of education and health services has rightly resulted from concern for human rights and dignity. In addition, good citizens must understand that access to education, improvement in its quality, adequate health services, racial desegregation, and freedom of mobility can add much to the strength of the nation. Aid for such measures, governmental or private, might do more for ultimate success in the cold war than equal amounts spent on weapons.

It is no accident that a state such as Mississippi—which contains fertile land and other rich natural resources—is at or near the bottom of the list of states in per-capita income, per-capita expenditure for schools, infant mortality, and number of physicians and dentists per thousand of population.

In this connection I have been reminded of a conversation with Sir William Beveridge during the last winter of World War II; Beveridge was a noted British economist who drew up for his government the plans for social insurance adopted immediately after the war. He had visited the United States and knew it well. Among my questions I asked what he thought should be emphasized in postwar planning in this country. He replied, "Increase in the incomes of people in your southeastern states."

Many volumes have been written on the need for more and better education throughout the nation, from nursery schools all the way to postgraduate studies. Adequate public support of schools, colleges, and universities can benefit not merely the individuals concerned but the strength of the nation. Dropouts from primary and secondary schools may become delinquent; in any case they increase the ranks of the unemployed because of lack of demand for unskilled labor.

Aside from formal education, operatives who have lost their jobs because of automation or the decline of industries in which they have worked need retraining and perhaps relocation. The bill must be paid by someone—usually government—because unemployment insurance, in many cases insufficient even for short periods of joblessness, runs out after a few weeks and leaves the victims without resources except those dedicated to charity. Here and there progressive and successful employers have made contracts with labor unions guaranteeing either that no employees on the payroll will lose their jobs as a result of gains in productivity, or establishing adequate pensions for those no longer needed. Practices of this sort, however, are not likely to become universal because industries or firms which are not prosperous and growing cannot afford them. Some comprehensive plan for diminishing "hard core" unemployment resulting from technological gains is essential.

Long-term Goals

Competition between the Western powers and the Communist nations in recent years has emphasized capacity for destruction. This rivalry proves little about gains under the respective social systems, each of which is supported by its adherents as the best way to serve human life. There are, in broad terms, just two alternatives open to the contestants and to the "uncommitted" peoples who are invited to join their camps. One is to continue absorption in the race for superior power to annihilate. The other is not to abandon the contest between the great rivals, but to change the methods of scoring their global game. Which one offers its people the more abundant and significant life? If attention of their citizens and rulers could be diverted to gains in the humane qualities of their respective civil performances, the fury which can lead only to disaster might before it is too late give way to an emotional substitute for mass killing.

Industrial production, the index of which served at the beginning of this chapter as a means of judging relative speed of the Americans and Russians in their race, is better than counts of nuclear weapons, but it is scarcely adequate and might become seriously misleading. In the first place, a large component of this index consists of weaponry and plays no role in the well-being of the citizens except as a threat to possible enemies.

In the second place, if production is to be used as an index of welfare, it ought to include not only products of manufacturing industries but also output of agriculture and fisheries. Most of the foods and fibers produced on farms or taken from the waters are processed, especially in the United States, and so do turn up eventually in the output of industry, but some are not; Russia especially depends on retail distribution of unprocessed foods.

A more important defect of the industrial-production index is that it does not cover the large and growing sector of nontangible services. In the United States services now constitute more than one-third of the gross national product and have been growing more rapidly than industrial output. The Soviet Union, following Marx's doctrine, does not record the contribution of services to national income. Services include, as major factors, such indispensable parts of production as education, medical and health services, and the work of governmental employees and elected officers engaged in providing not physical goods but other essentials of a tolerable civilization. All these *are* included in the gross national product of the United States.

Gross national product itself does not yet count qualitative gains (or losses) in man's search for a humane civilization. (Many of these are not susceptible to measurement by index numbers.) Among them are conquests of disease and gains in expectation of life, gains in modifying inequality of income, and improvement in working conditions. Has city and regional planning made any headway in conquering the blights of metropolitan centers or their suburbs? What about excellence in literature and the fine arts, which are the crown, if not the essence, of great societies? Of major importance is the administration of justice and the exercise of police powers in protecting citizens from crime or despotism. Rival social orders cannot be meaningfully compared without including consideration of such matters.

The Economy of Time

Industrial civilization has frequently been criticized by those who regret the loss of personal involvement in work because of the substitution of machines for skilled and creative craftsmen. Men and women subject to the system, under the authority of profit-seeking employers, have been pictured as robots. Yet the continued achievements of science and technology have made it possible for the employees affected to spend less time on their paid jobs and more in doing what they please. In generation after generation, while productivity of goods has been increasing, wage-earners have demanded, and received, not only more goods but more free time. With the new burst of productivity commonly attributed to automation, this historic trend is likely to be continued.

In the early period of the Industrial Revolution factory operatives worked six days a week and ten, eleven, or even twelve hours a day. Gradually, and often only after bitter struggles, labor gained the eight-hour day and the five-day week, and now is expecting the thirty-five-hour week. Many have achieved paid vacations.

One need not maintain that disastrous unemployment must result from the new electronic devices unless still shorter working hours are enforced. The new methods are capable of producing in the same time more real income in goods, which many will welcome. As need for hand-workers decreases, the need for designers, repairers, and operatives of the automatic devices increases. Shortening of working hours is probably not required to prevent growing unemployment. Nevertheless, many employees are likely to continue the historic trend of demanding at least part of their possible gain in free time and only part in higher real wages.

Free time is itself a precious gain for the individual. In the life of any one person, time is a commodity fully as scarce as the three standard scarce resources identified by traditional economic doctrines—land, labor, and capital. If free time is to be fruitful for either the individual or his society, it must be allocated by him with care for genuine needs and permanent values, as economists have always contended that scarce physical resources ought to be allocated. Time cannot be hoarded. There is already a large literature on the social and individual problems involved in the new leisure. It might in the end lead to as significant changes in human culture as historians have discovered in former epochs of civilization.[1] It might make over a majority of the citizens as members of "the leisure class."

Such an outcome was envisaged by the great British economist and philosopher John Stuart Mill (1806-1873), a contemporary of Karl Marx and a lay prophet who looked forward to a better society, as did Marx, but with keener foresight of what might happen. The quotations below are from Book Four of his *Principles of Political Economy,* the first edition of which was published in 1848, the year of the *Communist Manifesto.*

> I confess I am not charmed with the ideal of life held out by those who think that the normal state of human beings is that of struggling to get on; that trampling, crushing, elbowing, and treading on each other's heels, which form the existing type of social life, are the most desirable lot of human kind, or anything but the disagreeable symptoms of one of the phases of industrial progress....
>
> Those who do not accept the present very early stage of human improvement as its ultimate type may be excused for being comparatively indifferent to the kind of economical progress which excites the congratulations of ordinary politicians; the mere increase of production and accumulation.

Mill wished technological advance to continue in a future "stationary state," not for the purpose of accumulating material wealth, but to approach equalization of income and to create a society which contained "a much larger body of persons than at present, not only exempt from the coarser toils, but with sufficient leisure, both physical and mental,

[1] Reflections on that subject by this author may be found in *Time for Living* (New York: The Viking Press, 1955).

from mechanical details, to cultivate freely the graces of life."

> It is scarcely necessary to remark that a stationary condition of capital and population implies no stationary state of human improvement. There would be as much scope as ever for all kinds of mental culture, and more and more social progress; as much for promoting the Art of Living, and much more likelihood of its being improved, when minds ceased to be engrossed by the art of getting on. Even the industrial arts might be as earnestly and as successfully cultivated, with the sole difference, that instead of serving no purpose but the increase of wealth, industrial improvements would produce their legitimate effect, that of abridging labor.

Mill would also have urged the United States Congress of the 1960s to adopt the proposed legislation to set aside "wilderness areas." For the same reasons he also supported limitation of population growth. He wrote: "A population may be too crowded, though all may be amply supplied by food and raiment. It is not good for a man to be kept perforce at all times in the presence of his species. . . . Solitude in the presence of natural beauty and grandeur, is the cradle of thoughts and aspirations which are not only good for the individual, but which society could ill do without."

SELECTED REFERENCES

TO FOLLOW CURRENT FIGURES OF NATIONAL INCOME, EMPLOYMENT, PRODUCTION, AND OTHER ECONOMIC STATISTICS, CONSULT:

The Economic Report of the President. Washington: U. S. Government Printing Office, annually.

The Survey of Current Business. Washington: U. S. Department of Commerce, monthly.

The Federal Reserve Bulletin. Washington: Board of Governors of the Federal Reserve System, monthly.

Manpower Report of the President. Washington: U. S. Government Printing Office, annually, beginning 1963.

Statistical Abstract of the United States. Washington: U. S. Department of Commerce, annually.

FOR MORE DETAILED MATERIAL ON NATIONAL INCOME:

National Income Supplement to the Survey of Current Business. July 1947.

Kuznets, Simon. *National Income and Its Composition, 1919–1938*. New York: National Bureau of Economic Research, 1941.

———. *National Product Since 1869*. New York: National Bureau of Economic Research, 1946.

———. *National Income: A Summary of Findings*. New York: National Bureau of Economic Research, 1946.

Stigler, George J. *Trends in Output and Employment*. New York: National Bureau of Economic Research, 1947.

FOR THE BUSINESS CYCLE:

Mitchell, Wesley C. *Business Cycles: The Problem and Its Setting*. New York: National Bureau of Economic Research, 1927.

———. *What Happens during Business Cycles.* National Bureau of Economic Research. Published by Princeton University Press, 1950.

Moore, Geoffrey H., Ed. *Business Cycle Indicators.* Vol. I: *Contributions to Analysis of Current Business Conditions.* Vol. II: *Basic Data on Cyclical Indicators.* National Bureau of Economic Research. Published by Princeton University Press, 1961.

Business Cycle Developments. Washington: U. S. Department of Commerce, monthly.

Burns, Arthur F. "Progress toward Economic Stability." *American Economic Review,* March 1960.

———. *Economics and Our Public Policy of Full Employment.* New York: Morgan Guaranty Survey, published by Morgan Guaranty Trust Co., July 1963.

Clark, John J., and Cohen, Morris. *Business Fluctuations, Growth, and Economic Stabilization.* New York: Random House, 1963.

FOR ECONOMIC GROWTH:

Fabricant, Solomon. "Productivity, Its Meaning and Trend"; "Productivity and Wages"; "Productivity and Prices." New York, *Challenge,* October 1962, November 1962, December 1962. Institute of Economic Affairs, New York University.

Kendrick, John W. *Productivity Trends in the United States.* National Bureau of Economic Research. Published by Princeton University Press, 1961.

"Investment in Human Beings." Papers at a Conference of Universities—National Bureau Committee for Economic Research. Chicago, *The Journal of Political Economy,* October 1962.

Reducing Tax Rates for Production and Growth. New York: Committee for Economic Development, 1962.

Proceedings of a Symposium on Economic Growth. New York: The American Bankers Association, 1963.

Comments on the President's 1963 Economic Report. New York: The American Bankers Association, 1963.

FOR THE OPERATION OF THE BANKING SYSTEM:

The Federal Reserve System: Its Purposes and Functions. Washington: Board of Governors of the Federal Reserve System, 1947.

Freedman, Milton, and Schwartz, Arma Jacobson. *A Monetary History of the United States 1867–1960.* National Bureau of Economic Research. Published by Princeton University Press, 1963.

FOR THE KEYNES THEORIES:

Keynes, J. M. *The General Theory of Employment, Interest and Money.* New York: Harcourt, Brace, 1936.

Robinson, Joan. *Introduction to the Theory of Employment.* New York: Macmillan, 1937.

FOR INDUSTRIAL CONCENTRATION:

Smaller War Plants Corporation (Report), Economic Concentration and World War II. Washington: U. S. Government Printing Office, 1946.

Berle, A. A., and Means, Gardiner C. *The Modern Corporation and Private Property.* New York: Macmillan, 1933.

Chamberlin, Edward. *The Theory of Monopolistic Competition.* Cambridge: Harvard University Press, 1946.

Knauth, Oswald. *Managerial Enterprise.* New York: Norton, 1948.

Business Concentration and Price Policy (Conference Report). National Bureau of Economic Research. Published by Princeton University Press, 1954.

FOR THE INTERNATIONAL SITUATION:

Research and Planning Division, Economic Commission for Europe. *A Survey of the Economic Situation and Prospects of Europe.* New York: United Nations, 1948.

Cohn, Stanley H. *The Gross National Product in the Soviet Union: Comparative Growth Rates.* Washington: U. S. Department of Commerce, 1963.

Nutter, G. Warren. *The Growth of Industrial Production in the Soviet Union.* National Bureau of Economic Research. Published by Princeton University Press, 1962.

Lipsey, Robert E. *Price and Quantity Trends in the Foreign Trade of the United States.* National Bureau of Economic Research. Published by Princeton University Press, 1963.

The European Common Market and Its Meaning to the United States. New York: Research and Policy Committee, Committee for Economic Development, 1959.

Japan in the Free World Economy. New York: Research and Policy Committee, Committee for Economic Development, 1963.

Economic Impacts of Disarmament. Washington: U. S. Arms Control and Disarmament Agency, 1962.

Economic and Social Consequences of Disarmament. New York: United Nations Economic and Social Council, 1962.

INDEX

DR. WILLIAM K. WIDGER, JR.
RFD #2, Hillrise Lane
Meredith, N. H. 03253